What They're Saying ...

Dr. Judith Briles provides easy to understand advice on how to publish painlessly in *How to Avoid Book Publishing Blunders*. This is essential reading for all authors wishing to self-publish.
—Robin Cutler, President of worldwide LMBPN Publishing

Judith Briles has created a wonderful collection of 101 gems of book publishing wisdom. *How to Avoid Book Publishing Blunders* helps authors publish in print with greater pride, professionalism and success. Learn how to approach publishing as a business, avoid predators, and target and reach the right readers.
—Mark Coker, Smashwords founder

Judith Briles shows you how to avoid the most expensive and time-consuming mistakes that have haunted thousands of other authors. This book is like a combination safety net, burglar alarm and crash helmet. Buy it. Read it. Follow it. It will keep you out of trouble.
—Joan Stewart, The Publicity Hound

So much useful information
As a newbie to the world of publishing, this book is so helpful and is packed with lots of practical and useful information to help me get my book out. I am now listening to it again and have

bought the kindle to make full use of what I am learning!
—Amazon Reader Book Review

Judith Briles does it again, providing exactly the resource indie authors need to make their way through the publishing jungle. From planning to platforms to real-world strategies, this is the go-to guide that I'll be recommending.
—Joel Friedlander, Author, *A Self-Publisher's Companion*

If I had a nickel for every time a person called me and said, "I just spend $30,000 publishing and marketing my book and I have nothing to show for it. What can you do for me?" I'd take all those nickels and buy a zillion copies of this book and give them away. Authors would save a small fortune and will produce a much better book!
—Dan Janal, founder of PR LEADS and author of *Reporters Are Looking for YOU!*

Real World Advice in an Authentic Voice
Being new to writing novels, this book has been a terrific and practical guide. It's not too heady or scholastic to follow and Briles gives real-world advice in a way that feels more like it's coming from a good friend than another author. While I've never met her, I feel like it would be wonderful to sit and chat with her over tea and muffins. She outlines her 101 tips in an

approachable way and her down to earth voice is always with you, both encouraging and easy to understand. This has become a checklist and as I write, I always hear her, like a pal, keeping me on track. Highly recommend for any new author!
—Amazon Reader Book Review

If you are overwhelmed by the mountain of information (and misinformation) offered to independent authors, rest easy—this book will guide you through the maze. Judith Briles offers a tremendous amount of helpful content in a no-nonsense, quick-to-read style. She takes you by the hand 101 times, offering advice for the issues you knew about and problems you would never see coming without her help. Don't indie publish without this guide or the other titles in her *AuthorYOU Mini-Guide Series*.
—Michele DeFilippo, book designer and author of *Publish Like the Pros, A Brief Guide to Quality Self-Publishing*

Be a book publishing success
Invaluable information very comprehensive Everything I need to know to succeed all in one place. Covers things I would not have thought about. Kudos to Judith Briles as—she knocked it out of the park. I carry it with me wherever I go. It is my new 'American Express' card as I never leave home without it. I read it when I am in line wherever. On the highway, we call it road rage,

on the surface streets, e.g., stores, banks, retail establishments it is called 'line rage'. In line is an excellent time to read and keep calm. Again, thank you Judith Briles for an outstanding contribution in this very vital area called Book Publishing.
—Amazon Reader Book Review

Here's what I love about Judith Briles and this book: She gives it to you straight. No coddling. No B.S. She's the poster child for self-publishing tough love. Judith knows what will make a positive difference for authors and shares it in this gem that I will recommend to every author who asks me, "What do I need to know about publishing my book?"
—Sandra Beckwith, *BuildBookBuzz.com*

This little big book packs a powerful punch. As a book designer for over 25 years, Judith Briles answers many of the design, publishing and marketing questions daily thrown my way. If you're a serious author, this book needs to be on your desk—ESSENTIAL READING!
—Nick Zelinger, NZGraphics.com

Eye-opening advice for new writers
Judith Briles' *How to Avoid Book Publishing Blunders* is an easy pocket-sized read that will help countless beginning writers weave through

cover design, editing, copyright, ISBN and LCCN numbers, contract clauses to watch out for, and on and on. It makes a new writer realize that the steps involved in the manufacturing and printing of a book, and in achieving appropriate publicity in marketing it, will absorb much very worthwhile time and thought. To get these things right, get this book.
—Amazon Reader Book Review

Judith Briles knows her audience for sure! This guidebook perfectly encapsulates the questions we authors who write to help authors succeed get asked most often. And no one knows the answers better the Briles!
—Carolyn Howard-Johnson,
author of the multi award-winning
How To Do It Frugally Series of books for writers

Tremendous value
There is a staggering amount of information in here which I know would have cost me a great deal of time and money if I'd managed to learn it all the hard way. Some of the tips I knew already but wasn't necessarily putting into practice; the rest I didn't and am very grateful to be learning it now. Plenty of concrete, no-nonsense advice. It has made me get a lot more serious about publishing.
—Amazon Reader Book Review

How to Avoid Book Publishing Blunders

Dr. Judith Briles
The Book Shepherd

www.MileHighPress.com
MileHighPress@aol.com
303-885-4460

MileHigh Press

How to Avoid Book Publishing Blunders
© 2022 Judith Briles
All rights reserved.
No part of this book may be reproduced in any written, electronic, recording, or photocopying form without written permission of the publisher. The exception would be in the case of brief quotations embodied in critical articles or reviews and pages where permission is specifically granted by the publisher.

Portions of this book were published previously under the title of *How to Avoid 101 Book Publishing Blunders, Bloopers and Boo-Boos.* Every precaution has been taken to verify the accuracy of the information contained herein, the author and publisher assume no responsibility for any errors or omissions. No liability is assumed for damages that may result from the use of information contained within.

Books may be purchased in quantity
by contacting the publisher directly:
Mile High Press, Ltd., 8122 S Quatar Circle, Aurora CO 80016
or by calling 303-885-4460 or email MileHighPress@aol.com

Editing: John Maling, EditingByJohn@aol.com;
Peggie Ireland, TheBookShepherd.com
Cover and Interior Design:
Nick Zelinger, NZGraphics.com, Rebecca Finkel, F+P Design
Illustrations: Don Sidle, www.DonSidle.com

ISBN: 978-1-885331-89-2 (paper KDP)
ISBN: 978-1-885331-91-5 (paper IngramSpark)
ISBN: 978-1-885331-90-8 (eBook)
ISBN: 978-1-885331-62-5 (audiobook)
LCCN: 2016905299

1. Publishing   2. Self-publishing   3. Author   4. Reference

Second Edition   Printed in the United States

In memory of Dan Poynter
and Joel Friedlander ...
Friends. Publishing Visionaries. Truth Tellers.

CONTENTS

Author's Note 1

1 The Business of Publishing
  & Platforms 5

2 Publishing Predators 25

3 Publishing Service Contracts........... 41

4 Writing Smarts 63

5 Editing Musts........................... 83

6 Front Matter Must Haves................ 95

7 Cover & Interior Design................ 111

8 Printing Panache 131

9 eBook Ahas............................. 147

10 Social Media Moxie 159

11 Ninja Marketing 173

12 Blogging Power........................ 205

13 Publicity & PR........................ 215

14 Amazon Savvy.......................... 227

15 Bookstores............................ 239

16 This 'n That 247

17 Author Success	269
One More Thing	297
Cheat Sheet	299
Thanks to My Village	305
Meet Judith Briles, The Book Shepherd	311
Working with Judith	317

Author's Note

THERE ISN'T AN AUTHOR who doesn't have a list that starts with "Next time …" or "If I had it to do all over, I would …"

It is essentially an author and publishing bucket list of things to do "right" vs. snafus and mistakes along the way. We all make them, even those of us who have published many times.

Those blunders and mistakes—cost you money. Sometimes they are just small amounts of time and/or money; unfortunately, sometimes they are sizeable enough to literally knock you out of the playing field. Mistakes range widely. They are about working with the wrong people, getting on the wrong path, not planning, not being realistic, sometimes even low-balling what your real potential is. Mistakes can even easily suck you into publishing predator land. And, they can launch you into a misdirection, one you hadn't planned to go down.

Initially, I envisioned the *AuthorYOU Mini-Guides Series* opening with *Publishing Timelines*.

It didn't. Instead, *The CrowdFunding Guide for Authors & Writers* jumped ahead of what I planned. That happened on a Saturday morning during my monthly AuthorYOU coaching Salons that I hold in my home in Colorado. One of the participants was contemplating a crowdfunding campaign and was clueless as to what it took—how to even go about it. She, and others, needed a mini-guide. I wrote one, just for authors.

With that written and published, I thought I could turn my attention back to *Publishing Timelines*. Nope. Once again, between the monthly in-person coaching and the weekly phone coaching, there was another nagging topic that kept surfacing—mistakes. Those blunders that are common, not-so-common, costly and author-sucking mistakes.

Yikes, at times I wondered to myself—Why? Why are the same blunders, mishaps, snafus—you name it—keep bubbling up? Surely there is enough info on the Internet to shout out fair warning. There isn't.

Once again, *Publishing Timelines*, as did *Publishing Costs*, got pushed back. Author and book mistakes prevention was critical.

Authors had to avoid those perilous paths whenever possible. If the long laundry list of blunders wasn't put out, timelines didn't matter.

One of the biggest blunders is that authors don't treat their publishing as a business. It is. And they don't get how critical it is to start creating their INFLUENCE FACTOR—email building and social media presence.

Newbie authors can easily become overwhelmed. Old-timers can as well ... or they just get tired with all the "new stuff" that keeps gurgling up that they are told they "must do." Within *How to Avoid Book Publishing Blunders,* I've identified a variety of critical elements to publishing success that are unknown or ignored (or sometimes forgotten). Either way, there is a huge cost to authors.

Judith

P.S. One of the blunders that authors make is not asking for help. All authors want reviews, need reviews, of their work. Do this author a favor and post a review on Amazon for my book. Thank you.

The Business of Publishing & Platforms

Any author who desires to be successful needs to put on his or her big author pants. Learn the business elements around publishing. Dabbling and being a hobbyist will not move you forward. Platform building should start from the author's get-go. You seed it with your vision, your passion/enthusiasm and commitment.

Treat Authorship and Publishing as a Business

ARE YOU IN THIS for "something to do," or are you serious about being a success? Be clear on what it takes to break even. Just how many books do you have to sell to cover your initial expenses? Do you have a plan? Success in authoring rarely happens overnight. It takes time and patience along with any plan. It's your choice; you choose.

TIP: Publishing has a cost to it: the investment includes your time, your energy, and yes, your money. Start by getting educated. Hang out with authors who "are doing it" and identify who the top influencers are in publishing.

I'm not talking about the one-book wonder who is the current buzz or self-proclaimed guru. I'm talking about those who have some roots; have been at the game for years; experienced the roller coaster of ups and downs. In other words, they are seasoned and can talk the walk because they have really walked the talk. Follow their blogs, join their communities and make comments. Attend high-content conferences like the Unplugged events I do throughout the year online and in-person. You will find them under "Experiences" on *TheBookShepherd.com* website.

Do Your Pre-Work

IF YOU HAVEN'T DONE your pre-work to know what's out there in the bookstores and on the Internet, you are making a huge mistake. If you don't have your name, your topic, key phrases and topics registered on Google Alerts or Talk Walker, you get big demerits.

Bookstores, and the people who work in them, can be your best friend. Your authoring journey is the perfect time to become a familiar patron at your local bookstore—one of the biggies, like Barnes & Noble and one of the independents. I'm in Colorado—we've got a variety of excellent indies including the BookBar, Books Are Awesome, Boulder Bookstore and Old Fireside Books Use *IndieBound.org* as a portal with a zip code to find bookstores near you. I bet that there is something that is unique to you and your locale as well. Whatever is close, go. Get to know the personnel, the person who heads up the section/genre that your book would land in, and meet the manager.

For the developing and emerging author, experienced bookstore employees can offer some coaching: what's moving in the store; what colors are popping on covers; what type of books customers are asking for, or what types of problems customers are seeking solutions to; and what the local book clubs are reading and buzzing about.

Pay attention to what's happening within your genre. Whether it's in the news, in the blogs, or in your head, be prepared to focus when needed.

What you don't want to create is something that has become passé or just another cliché. Yes, things do go retro ... but if you are a nonfiction author, determine where the need is, figure out what has been done in the area, then do your version with a twist. For fiction, it's only your imagination that is the limit. How awesome is that?

TIP: Think of yourself as a universal sponge; what's hot, what's not. Get that publishing is a business. If you are a dabbler or a hobbyist, the odds of being successful are remote.

Create Author and Book Platforms

DO YOU KNOW WHAT ignites your *passion* for your topic? Have you created a vision for both you as the author and for your book? Have you really probed into your *commitment factor* in time, energy and yes, money? And, do you know who your *crowd* is? All these come into play when it comes to building a solid Platform for you and your book. Use ***Author YOU: Creating and Building Your Author and Book Platforms*** workbook as a guide that is available on Amazon.

The Internet has been a game changer for authors. With a few strokes, you may find a viral world that is chomping at the bit for your info and your stories. If you already have a following, you should be teasing them with "glimpses" of what's to come.

One of the most common mistakes authors make is not recognizing that book marketing starts within the Platform. Pre-launching a book long before it is out and available versus waiting until it is can make the difference between success and sputter.

TIP: Savvy authors not only let their crowd know that a book is in the works—they start the buzz. The Author and Book Platforms focus on who your book is for; where they hang out; what their communities are all about; and they set the stage for you to succeed. Your Platforms: don't leave home without them.

Not Having a Written Publishing Plan

WE ALL NEED SOME type of a guide for a project. Oh, you may have one in your head—which is good. Visualizing what your book will look like; feel like; seeing buyers line up to buy it; speaking from a stage to hundreds—heck, thousands, is always good. But, what's the plan in getting there? What are you doing to hold yourself accountable in bringing those crowds; delivering the book that will have the oohs and aahs gurgling forth? Yes, you need a PLAN.

If your goal is to publish via a traditional publisher, the proposal you will need to create will include information on marketing—your plan to shout out and implement buying. If you are publishing yourself, what's your plan for producing the book and marketing it? Do you have a plan to reach out to media for publicity?

Do you have a plan for educating yourself in the how-tos, nuances, and twists and turns of publishing?

If you are like most authors, you don't. You just want to get the book done and out. If that's your plan, get ready for disappointment.

TIP: Your PLAN should be to succeed. Therefore, your plan should be to have a PLAN ... and get it in writing. Your PLAN should have a beginning and an end. It should have room for flexibility. After all, some of the road bumps you will encounter along the way will need you to create alternate routes so you can get to the end ... book in hand. Your PLAN needs to keep WHO the audience is that you are writing for, front and center.

You can do it yourself ... or you can even hire it out ... but you better be joined at the hip with the person who is creating it. Your PLAN acts as a guide to what your book is about; who your market is; how you are going to reach out and connect with it; what media support you are going to desire and use; how much money you are going to invest in your venture; even, what kind of spin-offs you are thinking of. A PLAN with proper, step-by-step planning is essential to your publishing success.

When there isn't a PLAN, there really is one ... the PLAN is to *not plan*. Is that what you want? Not having a PLAN is a good way to practice the art of floundering and that will lead to failure.

Not Having Defined Your Goals That Includes Steps on How You Are Going to Reach Them

YOUR PLAN IS TO write and publish your book. Excellent. Now what are the steps you need to get there? They become your stepping stones across the broad publishing stream.

Those stepping stones are essential to identify from the get-go ... and know that you will have additional ones pop up as you progress. Your stepping stones should have measurements to them and dates when they will be achieved. Yes, hiccups can come in and bump them—but if you don't put timelines in play, next week becomes next month, sometimes next year.

When you have others who are contributing (who are they, what are they doing for you, what are their costs, when will they deliver to you, completed, what they are doing), they are one or more stepping stones to your success.

TIP: Your goal is to publish a book. *The first stepping stone is to write the book.* **What are the "stones" you need to write and complete it? These could include a place to write; times to write; things you need around you to write; how you are going to write and on what tool; what research needs to be done to support your book; possible "rewards" as you finish a chapter. I wrote an entire book with a bag of M&Ms as the reward when the first draft of a chapter was completed—geeze, I gained 10 pounds writing** *Stabotage!*.

You may need to declutter—I'm not saying throw things out—I'm referring to removing distractions that will get in your way (it could be visuals around you, TV, outside activities, you may need a social media and email diet—limiting yourself to much shorter times searching, playing, responding) ... anything that pulls you away from your mission of writing the book. What else could be on your stepping stone list to move you and your book forward?

For me, ideally, I need sun and water. I need hot cups of tea and in afternoons, lots of peach or mango iced tea. Sometimes I need some of my favorite music in the background. And, I need to be left alone when I'm in the zone. I write "binge" style ... not at a set time each day; rather in huge swoops of time—where most other things are blocked away. I write nonfiction— my research is done before I plunge in and I have printed out primary components of it, segregated into piles or files that I can quickly access and then refile when I'm done with them—out of sight.

When I'm in the writing zone and I'm in my inner offices in a comfy chair or outside on the deck where sunshine awaits me—my staff and family know: leave me alone. They also know I welcome food and drink—but otherwise, leave me alone until I surface. Other writing zones include away from home and office. I've started and finished books in Kauai and Maui (water and sun) and many a book was seeded and completed on the balcony of a cabin on a cruise (water and sun) as this one was.

Another step is to learn about publishing. What are the "stones" you need to get educated? Another step is to find an editor. What are the "stones" you need to find the right editor? You will need a cover designer. What are the "stones" you need to find the one that will best shout out your book in today's market and for your genre? You need an interior book designer. What are the "stones" you need to find—the ones that will best display your book for reading in today's market and for your genre? If your book will need illustrations or any art inclusions, what are the "stones" you need to find "the someone(s)" who will create the visuals that are the perfect fit? Et cetera, et cetera.

How are you going to get to your final goal? What stepping stones do you need? When do they need to be completed so you can continue to move forward? Write them out—they are critical and essential components to your author and book success.

Not Treating Authorship and Publishing as a Business

IT IS A BUSINESS, and a very big one at that. In 2020, over 750 million print books and 191 million ebooks were sold through through various online and brick and mortar outlets. These numbers don't represent books sold directly by authors/publishers on their websites or any direct sales outside of bookstores nor the number of audiobooks sold. That's huge moneys that are hitting bank accounts. Are you getting your share? For authors, it's imperative that you understand it is a business and what the business is.

Start learning the publishing business—the jargon, the basics, the how-tos. Attend conferences like the AuthorYOU Extravaganza and my Judith Briles Unplugged events. Hang out with authors who are doing what you want to do. Understand where the costs are and what your break-evens are from the get-go.

TIP: Understanding that publishing is a business—it's not a hobby—is critical. Grasping that early on will save you time and money. Your energy will be directed to learning steps and techniques that will save you thousands of dollars in mistakes down the road.

Goals are great ... but have you created the stepping stones to get you there? And, do you know when you arrive?

Will the shady individuals and companies who "service the publishing needs/wants of authors" ever drop into the abyss of hell? No, they are breeding, knowing that there is plenty of opportunity to tap into credit cards and bank accounts of ignorant authors-to-be. The savvy authors recognize the red flags, the lures that are thrown out, and check out who they deal with before engaging anyone. Moving from being naïve about the pay to publish crowd ensures a fast climb up the author success ladder.

Beware of Publishing Pitch Fests

BE CAREFUL OF WHAT is known as a "pitch fest." Pitched to newbie authors as education, they are really designed to lure them in (and their credit cards) to buy, buy, buy and buy some more. What are they buying? Products, services, trainings—you name it. Pitch fests are big business for the promoters. Authors want a quick fix to whatever ails them ... or they are on the hunt to the "wonder cure" for quick marketing success ... quick ways to get on TV ... *quick fill in the blank.*

Typically, the person running the conference gets half of the moneys. Such a deal ... for them. The truth is, is that too many attendees get emotionally hooked in the hype of the moment and buy with the herd when they shouldn't.

Suggestion: *Never pay for anything without using a credit card.* When the "hype of the moment" cools down and you are back home and realize you got roped in, that whatever you did is a wrong fit or not the right time for you, contact whoever hooked you and withdraw. Most likely you have a brief window to do this, such as three days. If that doesn't work, contact the credit card company and merely say that what you had initially bought was misrepresented to you and you want your money back. Companies like American Express and Bank of America move fairly quickly on their customer's behalf (that's you) and reverse the charges.

TIP: If you do land at a Pitch Fest, go in with a budget for yourself. I've seen some shell out mega-thousands with the deer-glazed look in their eyes. Pitch Fests will make you feel like the turkey "done" popper has popped up along with getting fannyitis as you sit through one pitch after another. It's a hype. Author Beware.

ARE THERE PREDATORS IN YOUR MIDST?

Don't Get Duped by "Self-Publishing" Companies

OK, MY HEART BLEEDS (yes it does—not to mention how ticked off I get) for the countless naïve authors who get sucked into these contracts. You pay moneys up front—often in the hundreds, then the cash register starts to vibrate—meaning your credit card. You need editing—you need illustrations—you need a press release—you need marketing—you need _____. By the time you are done, your "all it costs is $597 to publish your book" is now in the thousands and the results ... well, they are usually so-so at best and usually mediocre from the very beginning.

TIP: A book of any quality—I don't care if it's an "eBook" or print—print doesn't cost a few hundred bucks to create. Editing costs money. You shouldn't side step it. Your cover design should not look like your cousin Sammy did it; and your reader deserves an interior design that is appealing. Your book is an investment in YOU and your WORDS. Get educated.

Avoid the Seduction and "Come On" Lines Used by Publishing Predators ... "We will get your book distributed."

ONE OF THE MOST common is: *"We will distribute your print book to the largest bookstores."* Sure, authors would love to have their books in bookstores but—understand this—having a book available for distribution does not mean it lands on a shelf in a bookstore. *All it means is that it will land in the distributor's online catalogue.* Nothing more.

Authors today need to do a reality check. Bookstores have limited shelfing space. It's expensive real estate. Ask—is my book going to roll out of that store by the case ... or is it just going to hang out, hoping that a shopper discovers it? In the real world, most bookstores will take a pass on your book. Why? Two reasons: 1—the big publishers pay big bucks to have their books front and center (and it's still no guarantee that they will get sold); and 2—are you really going to work your tush off to drive all your potential buyers, followers, etc., to that bookstore or bookstore chain to discover and buy your book? Really?

TIP: Here's how to get "distribution" at zero to very minimal cost: Even if you are doing a traditional print run, set it up for for print-on-demand (POD) as well.

IngramSpark is Ingram, the granddaddy of book distributors—its online catalog is available to the great majority of all booksellers. When included in the Ingram catalog, your book can be found and ordered for a customer if it's requested.

KDP is Amazon. And KDP has created a variety of products within its frame that are excellent. The reality is that many bookstores don't want to order for customers because it's Amazon. But you are findable.

You can also pitch your book to Barnes & Noble. It has created a self-publishing portal on its website as well.

Don't be duped ... *You do not need to pay a self-publishing service company for this "service."*

The Great Lie: "We Are Your Doorway to Traditional Publishing"

THE BIGGEST VOICE FROM the vanity press – self-publishing crowd is Author House/Author Solutions. It's not uncommon for it or its reps to imply that when you sign with them you will get an inside track to traditional acquisitions editors. One of their classics is: "We are your doorway to traditional publishing."

Sounds good, but the odds are better at winning the lottery. As of this writing, the Author Solutions' website boasts of a "complete" list of authors who have made the leap—*less than 40 titles!* Let's do the math: Author Solutions claims to have helped authors publish 225,000 books. A lot of books, but when you crunch the numbers, it means a .015 percent success rate.

If you really want to be published with a traditional publishing house, then hone up your query writing skills and get an agent to pitch you and your book directly.

TIP: Self and independently published books are picked up by traditional publishers. If you book is selling well, or if it just happens to "fill a niche" a publisher is looking for, then you just might have a deal come your way. And if it does, take a bow. It will be due to your competent and savvy marketing, not those of the "self-publishing" company.

Savvy Authors Check Out Reputations of Publishing Providers

EVERY COMPANY, EVERY EDITOR, EVERY DESIGNER, EVERY CONSULTANT will have its share of unhappy customers. Face it, sometimes it just doesn't work out, so you are going to have to sort through any complaints you hear about or discover online to get a sense of which ones are legitimate. If you find multiple reports from unhappy customers, avoid that provider.

Tip: Do your homework before you commit. Websites like *Writer Beware, David Gaughran, and Alliance Independent Authors* are sources to check out as well.

Author Beware ... Scams, Cons and Predators Are in Your Midst

AUTHORS AND SELF-PUBLISHERS are routinely contacted by organizations offering "self-publishing services." What they are: "boiler rooms" of sales people making relentless calls—usually half way around the world. Persistence is their motto; their goal is your book-to-be and your credit card. And, they are experts at wearing you down and are hard to resist.

Be on alert. Be very careful. Don't get sucked in to the "special" of publishing your book for only $397, $497, $597 or whatever the "$97" number is. This is used as a lure to bring you in, then the "up sales" start. They are frequent advertisers in popular writing magazines (What better market to troll?) and it's not uncommon to create contests offering the grand prize of publishing the book of the winner or to offer free informational/how-to publish seminars or webinars—with the real objective of getting "new names" and contact info for the relentless callers to feast upon.

Some of these companies have tarnished records with a lot of unhappy customers. Several authors have complained to the Better Business Bureau and some have been sued. When people are victims of scams, they may report the incidents on the Internet. Before doing business with POD publishers or any other person or company that wants your money, make a Google search for:

(person and/or company name) + Scam
(person and/or company name) + Fraud
(person and/or company name) + Rip-off
(person and/or company name) + "Better Business Bureau"
(person and/or company name) + con
(person and/or company name) + complaints
(person and/or company name) + lawsuits

TIP: Some 90 percent of all Google searches stop at the first page—even though there are many items available to a searcher. DON'T STOP. Predators and cons know this and can "pepper" social media with faux reports, items, even posts about how great they are. The purpose is to drive any negative items deep from the first page of a Google search. Read everything. Read deep. Websites, such as *Writer Beware and Ripoff Report are* are excellent resources.

> *https://RipoffReport.com*
> *https://WriterBeware.com*
> *http://AbsoluteWrite.com/forums*
> *http://RipoffReport.com*

Publishing Service Contracts

Knowing what the fine print says; knowing about escape and termination clauses; knowing how to engage the ideal editor, designer, printer, illustrator or any other publishing service provider will enhance the professionalism and attract the buying crowd for your book. Most come with some kind of contract—understand what you are getting into and how you can get out, if necessary.

Don't Sign Any Contracts Until You Understand What You May Be Signing Away with a Traditional Publisher

AUTHORS WHO SIGN PUBLISHING related contracts for a contract to create/produce/sell their book through a traditional publisher should not jump in until they really understand the water. That means every clause; every paragraph. No exceptions.

TIP: If you don't "get" what it says, engage an attorney who specializes in intellectual property. Too many authors let their egos rule ... as in "I have a publishing contract ... a publisher wants my book" ... and they are clueless as to what they are getting into. For one, the publishing contract most likely isn't a contract that has the author's best interests.

It's designed for the publisher. And for that matter, the publisher may not be a true publisher. It could be a "pay to publish" operation ... meaning you pay for every service along the way. The risk is totally in your corner. It is well worth the expense to get someone's eyes on it who is an expert in intellectual property.

Only Sign a Contract with a Publisher to "Publish" Your Book if It Includes a Reversion of Rights Clause

WHAT'S THAT, YOU ASK? Simply this: in the "old days," traditional publishers included a *Reversion of Rights clause in contracts with authors.* What it did was enable the author to request that ALL rights revert back to him or her under certain conditions, basically terminating the contract for the book. The most common condition was dwindling to no sales. Today, that clause is as common as finding a T-Rex in your local neighborhood.

Many of the new breed of paid-to-publish companies include a clause about termination ... be very beware here. Avoid any that have a clause that states something along the line: You can terminate your contract with a 30 day notice if it's mutually agreeable. Mutually agreeable? You've got to be kidding. If you want out, you want out. The "mutual" can hold you hostage indefinitely.

татTIP: Because of POD, any publisher can keep a book "in print" in perpetuity. Ugh. Make sure you include your own version of a Reversion of Rights ... meaning that if your total print sales within the year are less than a specific number, such as 300 copies, that you have the right to terminate the contract. Make sure anything you sign with those you work with has an escape clause. Know what strings are attached to working with them BEFORE you go forward. You will thank me!

Always Include a First Right to Remainder Books Clause in a Traditional Publishing Contract

IF YOU SIGN WITH a traditional type of publisher and the contract is terminated for any reason, make sure you have a clause in your contract that *allows you to have first rights to any remainder books.* This should allow you to purchase books in inventory at a deep discount. Then, WOOT to you—you can resell with more money back to you. I like that!

You will want to document what the beginning inventory is. If your statement doesn't reflect it, ask and get the answer in writing. What are the sales for the reporting period? Are the sales increasing or decreasing?

TIP: It's important to pay attention to sales and inventory when your books are published. Typically, a publisher who prints an offset run places the books in its warehouse of choice. Those in turn are shipped to bookstores and distributors. As the author, you are usually behind the sales time, rarely knowing what true book sales are. Publishing companies usually report to the author twice a year and often three months after the closing period.

Don't Agree to Any Publishing Service You Don't Understand

NEVER SIGN A CONTRACT for a publishing service until you understand what the contract really says and that you have checked out the provider with others who have used the services.

TIP: Your essential question to ask anyone when you are gathering references: *Would you use this person or company again?* **If there is any hesitation, run. If they say "no" … ask why not. You and I both know that some people just don't click. That wouldn't scare me. If they do crappy work, that's another thing.**

Never, Never, Never Use Music Lyrics without Getting Written Permission

SONGWRITERS AND MUSICIANS DON'T give their words away. You may have a favorite line from *Yesterday* by Paul McCartney ... but you will be "yesterday" if you don't get written permission to use it or any of the lines. In 2016, he launched a bid to regain control of his share of the Beatles' catalogue's US publishing rights from Sony / ATV Music Publishing. Although he co-wrote the majority of the legendary band's hits, McCartney has never actually controlled the publishing. You would have to pony up some bucks to use anything from his or the Beatles' work in your book.

To obtain permissions, you can seek out someone who specializes in tracking down the rightful owners to get a price for you. You can also spend some time in a search engine doing the same thing. One of my clients wanted to use a few lines from the song *Monday Monday* by the Mamas and Papas. I was able to nail down the true owner and location within two hours—sent a letter with an exact copy of how the lines would be used in two chapters. Within a few weeks, a response came in with a fee of $150 for up to 10,000 copies of the book. This worked for the author.

TIP: Using any musical lyrics without permission is a lawsuit waiting to happen. You don't need one.

Caution Alert: Before You Sign Any Contracts ...

NEVER SIGN A CONTRACT for a publishing service until you understand what the contract really says and that you have checked out the provider with others who have used the services. Key question to ask when speaking directly to someone who has engaged them before: *Would you use this person or company again?* If there is any hesitation in the response, run.

Before signing ANYTHING, always do a Google search with the name of the person and company followed by the words: problems, complaints, ripoff, lawsuit, publishing predator, concerns, misrepresentation.

Make sure you dig past the first five pages. The truth is the great majority of those doing online searches rarely go past the first page of what comes up. Companies and people who get grumbles know the trick of pumping out a lot of postings with key words and phrases and push them to the top of the searches. The bad news continues to drop. Do your homework.

TIP: Don't let your ego guide you. Yes, you want a book. Contracts are usually written on behalf of the person giving it to you— not on your behalf. Don't leap until you understand what you are really jumping into.

Before Signing Any Contract, Determine How to Terminate It

Anytime you enter into a contract, any contract, you want to know what's in the divorce clause—if there is one, and there should be. After all, not all relationships work, whether they are personal or in business. You, your book and those you engage to get it created and published are no different. Some will have it stated that they have the rights to THE WORK for the life of the work. On the other end of the spectrum, many will say it can be terminated with a 30 day notice.

With self-publishing companies, they may allow termination but with strings attached, i.e. it has the right to sell any remaining inventory post the termination date and then it's over.

But, and it's a big but, how is the termination handled AND does it have any definitions to it? Some will say that the relationship ends via an email notice within a specific timeframe (make sure you copy yourself within the email and save it to your files); some require a certified letter (I would suggest you eliminate it and sub in an email notice). Whatever the process for termination, follow it and keep copies.

No company should have the right to continue printing your book and selling it after you terminate your relationship. That includes foreign rights.

TIP: If terminating with a self-publishing company, get the inventory count the date you announce the termination and check again 30 days later. Make sure the Amazon page and old eBook come down immediately. During the "30-day" transition, have a new eBook made, create your own Amazon page so you are back in the online book selling option.

**Before you sign ....
Know how to terminate!**

Before You Sign a Contract with a Self-Publishing Company, Know Ownership of Your Files if You Terminate

MOST WILL TELL YOU that any files created under their umbrella are theirs. Not necessarily so. Make sure you clearly understand the perimeters of your rights as the author, including how to end a contract and what you have the rights to, especially in cover and interior design. The reality is that you have PAID for these elements—get them. Be sure legal terminology protects them for you. Lawyer wording can be confusing.

TIP: Make sure your contract states that if you terminate, it will give you the final production-ready files of your cover and

interior at no or low cost (if there is a cost, get it in writing from the beginning of the contract). You want and formally request in the contract the actual and fully functional production files in *Adobe InDesign, Quark* or comparable format (these are the industry layout standards used by designers). If you don't get the rights to the files, it means you would have to recreate book files from scratch in order to work with another printer.

Know the Difference Between Exclusive and Nonexclusive Contracts

DON'T GIVE EVERYTHING AWAY. Yes, I get it. You are thrilled that a publisher (or anyone) is interested in your book. Breathe and know what you are letting others do with your work. When it comes to the self-publishing companies (the ones that you pay to publish your book), do not, do not, do not give EXCLUSIVE anything, which means file/screen/TV rights, subsidiary rights, rights to subsequent work, electronic rights, NOTHING.

TIP: Business attorney Helen Sedwick (*HelenSedwick.com*) and author of the *Self-Publisher's Legal Handback* advises that you only want to consider signing exclusive with a traditional publisher—one that pays you

a reasonable advance that shows it has an investment in you and your work. Companies that you are paying to manufacturer your work are not entitled to have the rights to any of your work. That means you retain ALL rights.

Your rights and your words could be in jeopardy. When in doubt, get independent advice. Don't let the promise of countless book sales get in your eyes.

What's In a Contract? ... It May Not Be What Provider Says

AUTHORS ARE SO EXCITED when a "deal" is offered that in reality, few really read their contracts, signing them blindly in their enthusiasm. Don't. If there is ever a time to engage a few hours of an intellectual attorney's time, a literary contract is it. Contracts are created for the benefit of a publisher or publishing service provider. Don't be fooled.

Tip: Don't sign anything until you read it, ask questions and make sure you understand it. When in doubt, get a consult pronto with a business or intellectual property attorney.

Writing smarter, writing wiser and writing to and for your crowd pushes the button to start gathering SuperFans. Learning and then embracing the fact that blogs, articles and books can begin a new life with a twist and tweak, repurposing old content into a new format. Understanding that headlines need a snap, crackle and pop element to them will make you a better writer and marketer.

Create a System That Quickly Identifies the LATEST File to Work/Write In

TOO OFTEN, AUTHORS GET files mixed up. They rewrite, delete and add to files that should have been archived. The wrong ones are "resent" to editors, designers, reviewers.

TIP: Create a "folder" within your working book folder. What you label it is up to you: OLD Files, NON-WORKING Files, DO NOT USE Files ... whatever works for you. After finishing with an old file—MOVE IT to this folder and add the date. This eliminates confusion and the possibility of reworking on discards plus the real chance of sending wrong files to a designer or editor. Only keep your CURRENT WORKING file easily available to you.

Your Voice in Your Writing Needs to Be Strong

FIRST ... **BE CONSISTENT.** SECOND ... **don't be passive.** In writing nonfiction, you are writing to an audience with your sage advice, help, how-tos and/or solutions. Avoid writing with the "WE" thing. Write with "we" when it's a joint writing: *we recommend*. Otherwise, it's *I recommend you* ... or *I recommend that* ... Your reader is the YOU ... your audience who is chewing on your words. You are delivering guidance to them. Yes, in some cases, literally taking the reader by the hand.

TIP: When you write in a passive voice; you open the "maybe" window. You want your reader to "take action."

Avoid Hyphen, en-dash and em-dash (ndash and mdash, n-dash and m-dash) Confusion

The use of dashes is inconsistent in lots of writing—regardless of who the writer is (amateur or long-timer). The hyphen, em-dash and en-dash crop up all the time while you're using Microsoft Word, but most don't know why and we use the different dashes inconsistently.

What's the visual difference between the en-dash and em-dash?

The "n-dash" is about as wide as an uppercase N; the "m-dash" (or em-dash) is as wide as an M.

Hyphen	-
en Dash	–
em Dash	—

An **en-dash** is used to connect values in a range or that are related. A good rule is to use it when you're expressing a "to" relationship.

- in years 2001–2010
- pages 63–66 are relevant
- The Denver Broncos smother the Carolina Panthers in 24–10 win

An **em-dash** is typically used as a stand-in for a comma or parenthesis to separate out phrases—or even just a word—in a sentence for various reasons.

- School is based on the three Rs—reading, writing and 'rithmetic.
- Against all odds, Martha—the unluckiest woman in love—discovered the love of her life.
- I sense something—a feeling I've not felt before.

A **hyphen** separates syllables of a word in a line break and is used to make a compound word; to avoid confusion or awkward spelling; to join letters and words; and numbers in a fraction.

- pro-America
- caged-free eggs
- self-publishing

TIP: You can create both the en-dash or em-dash quickly in Microsoft Word as well as the ever present hyphen.

en-dash: **Automatically created in Word when you type "something – something"** *(word-space-hyphen-space-word).*
em-dash: **Automatically created in Word document when you type "something—something"** *(word-hyphen-hyphen-word).*

Are You Boring, Politically Correct or Are You Cheeky in Your Headlines?

ALL HEADLINES ARE DESIGNED to get attention. Blah doesn't work. Ever. Savvy authors learn early on that when they move from using "safe" headlines, the faster they get attention. Using words that tap into the emotions or the outrageousness of readers become the grabbers that lead to openers. Which would you open first? ... *Learn about Blogging* versus *Five Essential Tips Busy Authors Must Use When Blogging*. They both really mean the same, but I bet the open rate will be 90 percent ahead with the second headline. After all, *essential busy* and *must use* are all attention grabbing.

TIP: Would you like to create one with some snap, crackle and pop? I'm always on the lookout for tools that will stir up my creative juices. During my annual three-day summer event, *Judith Briles Book Publishing Unplugged***, one of the days is spent on Gizmos and Gadgets—identifying, demonstrating and then implementing a variety of Tools, Tips and Tricks for Busy Authors.**

Three of my favorite tools that always generate responses from "cool" to "this is awesome" for boosting the power of headlines and titles include:

1. *TweakYourBiz.com* – Title Generator

Get ready to have your eyes opened. Inserting your key words or topic into the submission box will increase your open-up rate for a variety of usages, including social media posts. For "book publishing," *Tweak Your Biz* came up with Lists, Questions, Best, How to, even Snarky. More than a dozen categories and 100 plus suggestions were displayed in seconds. Most likely, many will be tossed … but *Book Publishing on a Budget: 5 Tips from the Great Depression* might create some pull.

2. *Portent.com* – Idea Generator

Get ready to have a little fun with Portent. It creates a variety of twists and turns, even goofy … but hey, sometimes goofy may be the perfect hook. Portent's process is simple: don't use upper case unless it's a proper name; use the singular version of your keyword; and keep revising to create a grammatically correct headline that is often a laugh-out-loud one.

My keyword phrases often have "book" or "publishing" in them. When I inserted "book publishing," one of the options was *Why Book Publishing Is More Tempting than a Cinnabon*— sounds delicious. I don't know about you, but comparing book publishing to munching on a Cinnabon wouldn't normally be something that I would think about for a title hook. But, millions enjoy Cinnabons weekly and the odds are many of them are authors or authors in the making— my market.

3. *AMInstitute.com* – Headline Analyzer

Created by the Advanced Marketing Institute, the Headline Analyzer is an excellent way to "goose" up your emotional pull with the reader. Step 1 is to enter your "working title"; Step 2, click on a category; and Step 3, submit for analysis. As you tweak your words, you will note the percentage of emotional marketing value change, or in some cases, disappears because there's no emotional pull for what you entered.

The higher your score using the Headline Analyzer, the probability of an open rate accelerates. Ideally, you would like to pull a score of 40 percent or higher. Most copywriters and headline pros will do a happy dance when they hit that magic percentage.

Note: any punctuation will be removed by its software when the results of the analysis are revealed. Just add it back in for your copy.

There Is a Goldmine in Repurposing Content ... Are You?

THERE IS NO REASON to create/invent new-new material for every social media platform or product you put your fingers on. A book that was written a few years ago can be cut up, combined with new information and re-introduced—new title, new ISBN, new descriptions, new cover—just new-new, all seeded with words that you created long ago. Now modified, your book has been repurposed.

Let's look at blogs. If you take a blog post or an article you wrote a few years ago, even a few months ago, it can be dusted off and with a make-over, re-used. How so, you ask?

- Create an audio clip for each blog post using a service such as *Audioboom*.

- Connect your Audioboom account to iTunes and start creating your own mini-podcast.
- Post them to your social media accounts. Also add clips to your website.

People like receiving information in short "bits and bites" so target audio clips to be about two to a maximum of five minutes in length.

- Another method to repurpose blog posts is to create boards on *Pinterest* for topics related to your blog posts. Weekly, I do a "tips" blog on *TheBookShepherd.com* website: the *Kick-butt Author and Book Publishing Tips and Ahas.* To repurpose it, a *Pinterest* Board was created for Author and Book Publishing Tips. Within the board, each tip then has a poster created and added. Done.

- Create a new Board, let's say Expert Tips on Book Marketing; add an image from the original blog that was posted along with a brief description of that blog post and include the URL to that blog post on your *Pinterest* Board. It's now linked.

- *YouTube* is next. Have you thought about taking your blog and creating a video? You've got the words already done. Blogs are usually short and can be presented on a video in just a few minutes. Programs like Camtasia can be used; the cameras on tablets and iPads can be put to use; and even your phone to get your feet wet.

"There's gold in them thar contents!"

TIP: Repurposing previously used material is smart. In fact, there could be another book by just combining a few of your blogs and articles. Themes and topics that have multiple postings are ideal to gather. Create

a new Intro for them, and exit with a type of call to action. Of course, include a a page to reference your other publications and one on how to connect with you via your social media channels and an inclusion of any services—consulting, speaking, etc.—that you provide. A new book is in your midst, created from the repurposing fairy dust.

Not Checking Your Writing Before Sending to Editors

WHEN YOUR READER NEEDS to go to the dictionary to figure out a meaning; when your sentences go on and on; when you use too many adverbs; when you forget that you have the "five senses" to use within your writing; and when your writing is way above the accepted norm grade level for your genre, you need some help. Not getting it before you bring in the editors is going to cost you in time and money.

Is your writing passive? Is it too complex? Is there another word that can be used that offers clarity to what you are writing? You may have a crossword puzzle vocabulary, but most people don't. There are plenty of tools—some for a fee. Find a tool that works for you and make it a habit; make it your stealth writing companion.

TIP: To the rescue is the Hemingway app, a terrific freebie that will make your writing bold and clear—transitioning from passive to active.

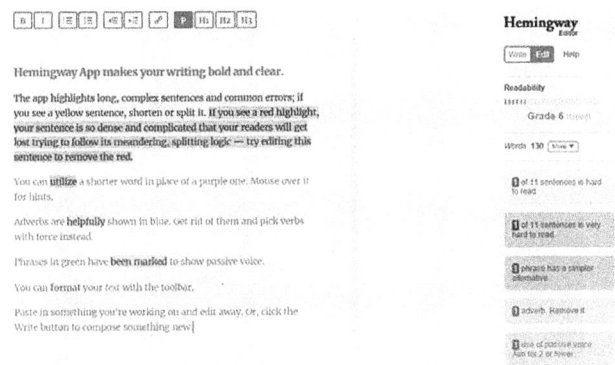

Suggesting replacement words, it gives you an immediate overall readability grade. The multi-purpose software highlights hard-to-read sentences (along with very-hard-to-read ones as well) in different colors. All you need to do is a "copy and paste" into the software once you download it. Easy peasy.

Learning to write well is a cycle. Most writers suck in the beginning. As they write more, they suck less. As they suck less, they write more. As they write more, they write better. As they write better, they write more. As they write more, the write faster. As the write faster, they write more.
As they write more, their words begin to sparkle.

Editing Musts

Grammar gremlins love your words, typos, verb confusion and paragraph perpetuity. The #1 mistake new and old authors make is the lack of editing. It's not your neighbor, your friend, your sister or your school English teacher who you engage. Editing starts with you on the first round; round two should bring in the professionals. Your book will thank you and your readers will cheer.

Use Professional Editors

THE DIFFERENCE BETWEEN most self-published books and small, independent and traditional publishing can be summed up in one word: editing … or the lack of it. If your book is loaded with errors, the odds are that you've lost the reader by page three.

Not all editors are the same. Ones that do *copy/proof editing* (grammar and typos) may not be the same as editors who are *content and developmental editors.* Content and developmental editors are word doctors. Their goal is to make your words, phrases and ideas pop. They will cost more than a copy editor. In many ways, they become a quasi-ghost for you.

One of the final things that you should do, before you print or move to an "e" format is to make sure that you print your book out, after the content/developmental editing has been done; after the copy/proof reading has been done; and after the book has been "formally" layed out. Why? Simply this: it is amazing what is still there. Yes, there are still typos; yes, punctuation that has run amok; yes, dropped words; and yes, there are still mistakes.

The third type of editor I bring in is what I call *the cold-eye editor—a proof reader*. The difference is that most proof readers read/go through the book *after* the editor does. Mine does as well—but it's done post layout, meaning a cold-eye editor is viewing the book in the exact format that the completed book will be in. She or he prints the book out from the designer and sits down to read from cover to cover—just as you envision your reader doing. It's essential that this person not had their eyes on your book before. In my offices, they know a title will come their way and an estimated time to expect, but that's it. *Why?* you ask. Because if he or she have done any work on your book, the odds that they will skim over and/or miss those hiccups—whether minor or major—increase significantly. Fresh eyes are what you want.

Amazingly, even with all of the eyes working on the book, the cold-eye editor returns the book with what we call "good catches" being found. Oh, commas are going to be there (or the lack of them); periods missing; lines get disconnected, etc.

But the truth is that your other editors and you have been in the book so long that you think things are there and they aren't; or you simply read over a glaring mistake because your mind tells you all is fine; or that a missing word is just automatically dropped in as you read it. The cold-eye editor is essential on my team. This is the final step before going to print.

TIP: Don't forget, editing flows to your cover and dust jacket copy as well. As Barbara McNichol says, "Don't skip the editing stage. And that doesn't mean turn to an English major friend. Solid copy/content editing that whacks wordiness and streamlines word choice makes your writing *sing*." If you want a professional book, get a professional editor involved—not your cousin Charlie who loves to read or your

mom, who was a school teacher. Choose an individual who edits for a living.

Tune your awareness level to some of these typical blunders:

- Be prepared for multiple drafts of your books. Too many authors think the first draft is it—then send it to the editor. What you are asking for is someone to rewrite your book. That's not what the editor does. You do the rewrites, then send it to the editor for the fine-tuning.

- Editors are human; they miss typos and grammar issues as well. Don't rely solely on yours for perfection.

- Don't be fooled into thinking you are the solo editor or your friend or relative is. Get someone in who does editing of your type of book for a living.

- Once you have had your book edited, now go through it again, line by line, for another read through. You will tweak, add/delete—guaranteed; there are always more changes.

- Make sure that your proofreader is not the same person who did your editing. You need new eyes.

Always Include a "Cold Eye" Final Edit

TYPOS, MISSING PUNCTUATION, EVEN a dropped or broken line can easily slip into the document that goes to the printer. What's a dropped/broken line? Here's one:
As the AUTHOR, you are responsible for the final approval. Always.

Obviously, "you are responsible ..." should follow AUTHOR, on the same line. But sometimes, in layout, a "drop or break" occurs.

I had a client who was absolutely sure that he had identified all edits needed in the final round to the degree that we had a bet that I would find not one, but several tweaks from the Cold Eye—100 bucks was on the table. We had a lovely dinner on him, as he just shook his head.

To prevent the "OMG, there are still mistakes in my book," you should:

- One … Always have one more read that does not include the original editor. In all the books that we handle in The Book Shepherd's offices, we do what we call the *Cold Eye Edit*. It's done only when the book has been formally layed out and read by one of our editors who has never seen the book before. It's given to her in only a hard copy format. It will absolutely not be proofed on any monitor, rather book in hand, as if one was reading it fresh from the bookstore shelf.

- Two … The Author is totally responsible for reading through the book one more time as well and told to read it out loud—word-*by*-word. Whoever did the original editing is out of the loop at this point.

- Three … When the "proof" is sent back to the author from the printer—be it POD or offset—the Author is responsible to once again read it printed out. It is the last gasp before the "ready" button is pushed.

TIP: Don't miss the final "peace of mind" step. It may cost you a few hundred dollars if you spot necessary changes, but it is worth every penny.

Get an Editor ... Pronto

NO EXCEPTIONS, ALWAYS ... ALWAYS ... Always use an editor who "gets" your genre. Your editor is a critical investment to the success of your book. You may need a developmental or content editor. That means that there is heavy re-writing and structure needed for your book. You may need copy editing—meaning that there aren't serious hiccups, just line editing to fix grammar, spelling, etc. Costs will vary depending upon what is needed. Developmental/content can be pricey—in many cases, that editor ends up doing heavy duty ghosting to fix the book.

Do you and your book a favor and have a "cold eye" final edit done POST layout—you will be amazed what pops up after a book is created as a book would be printed. Punctuation that was missing; words that were dropped (or never there but you and the editor had been in the book so many times that your minds just read them as if they were); lines that might have been dropped in layout.

For me, the Cold Eye is part of your book's secret sauce: the elimination of obvious and not so obvious snafus in your text and layout reflect poorly on you—the author.

TIP: No exceptions. All authors need editors—men and women who do editing for a living. Not your friend who teaches English or your favorite relative. Those people are readers—not editors.

Front Matter Must Haves

It's alphabet book soup time: ISBNs, CIP, LCCN, Copyright page, Dedication, Title page, Praise/Endorsement page and Content info; all set up your words, your story, your awesome insights, ahas and solutions. Make sure you have the right stuff in the right place. It's what Front Matter is all about.

Endorsements ... Do You Seek or Take a Pass?

SOME BOOKS NEED ENDORSEMENTS, some don't. Decide early on if they will help push your book out there. If they will, create a wish list of the ideal endorser(s). You want someone who has credibility within your genre—someone who brings clout with his or her name and is recognized by your potential buyer.

It's wise to steer clear of names that carry negative baggage. Most politicians do; so do some celebrities. You could instantly delete half of your potential buyers with the wrong choice. On the other hand, if one is publicly connected to an issue that your book highlights, it might be a perfect fit. It's homework time.

Outside of your personal contacts, you may have to reach out to those in your circle and ask: Who do you know who knows _____? Or, another great resource to use when you are seeking the "well known" is *The Celebrity Black Book.* Loaded with addresses and contact information, I need to forewarn you that it's pricey. Best bet is to go to Amazon and get a used one that is one or two years old for a fraction of the cost.

One of the things too many authors do in our Internet era is assume that potential endorsers desire to receive your book via an email link. Don't assume anything. You need to ask your potential cheerleaders how they would like to get your manuscript (or it could be an advanced reader copy—an ARC). Do they want an email attachment of a PDF? Word document? A printed out copy mailed? A sampling of chapters and *Contents* page? In other words, make it easy for them.

When I'm approached, the last thing I want to read is another book on my screen. Don't email me a manuscript. I tell my author-to-be I want a completed copy mailed to my offices with a time frame that I need to respond within.

If you are fortunate to get multiple shout outs, use them. Add all of your endorsements to the front matter of your book—have the interior book designer add them to the opening pages before the title page. After being lured by the cover, your potential buyer moves to the back cover and reads it. The next move is either to scan the interior and see how the book is visually layed out and/or to look at the endorsements on the first few pages, if there are any. It's what the big boys do in publishing, so why not you?

TIP: Don't forget to add endorsements to your website as well as to your Amazon pages.

If You Want Your Books in Libraries, Get a CIP Block

WHAT'S A CIP BLOCK? Glad you asked. The Cataloging in Publication record (aka CIP data) is a bibliographic record prepared by the Library of Congress for a book that has not yet been published. Contrary to what many authors and small publishers believe, it is not possible to get a CIP directly from the Library of Congress if your book is POD (print on demand), published by a press with less than three authors or is underwritten by the author. There's a way around this. To make sure your CIP data is in the appropriate form, there are vendors ready to pitch in. Through *AuthorU.org*, members are able to get a discount from the Donohue Group. It's website is *www.DGIInc.com*

TIP: Libraries want publishers to have CIP data. It shows that when you get it, you are a serious publisher—not a one-book pony.

Don't Bypass Using an ISBN on Your Book That Embeds the Price

IF YOU PLAN ON SELLING your book to a brick and mortar store or online store, you need an ISBN—no exceptions. A retailer wants the barcode representing the digitized ISBN number on the back of the book—with the price embedded within it.

OK, pick up a book, any book that you have purchased or is easily accessible. Note the barcode. It has a series of numbers that start with 978. Today's ISBN has 13 digits. To the right (or below) of the 13 digits will be a "5", then three or four additional digits—that's the price of your book. A book that retails for $18.95 will read: 51895.

Now, you may be thinking, I want to sell it for less at a conference. Fine, sell it for less. Just because the embedded price is $18.95 doesn't mean that you can't offer "special pricing" outside of a retail store.

my memoir *When God Says NO* is: 978-1-885331-76-2 and the price is $20.00.

TIP: If the barcode isn't price specific, most retailers will give it a thumbs down—"it" meaning you won't be selling there. Don't forget—include the ISBN for all versions of your book on the copyright page of the front matter: print, eBook and audiobook. That way, your copyright page will happily serve all formats.

Don't Get Just ONE ISBN ... Get At Least 10 ISBNs

IN THE US, BOWKER is your only legit source. Go to *http://www.MyIdentifiers.com.* In countries outside of the United States, determine who the appropriate supplier is via a quick Google search.

As of 2022, one ISBN is $125; 10 are $295. As soon as you pay online, you will receive your numbers within minutes via email. If you are a member of *AuthorYOU.org*, you can get a discount. 10 for $250. You will need an unique ISBN for each version of your book that you will produce: hardback (casebound), trade paper (softcover), trade paper with flaps, paperback, eBook and audiobook. If you have new editions, a new ISBN will be used.

TIP: Purchase at least 10, even consider 100! When you start thinking of all the variations of a book: hardback, paper, "e", audiobook, etc ... then there are new editions, spin-offs of the first book into other books. You can gobble up 10 ISBNs quickly.

Register Your ISBN So Retailers Can Find Your Book

TOO MANY AUTHORS THINK that just having the ISBN is all they need. Nope, you need to take another step. Yes, you buy them through R.R. Bowker and most likely the *MyIdentifiers.com* website. That's the first step. Now, you need to go back in and get specific. Report to R.R. Bowker the exact title that you are assigning to each ISBN you use.

This opens your title(s) up to free listings in Books in Print, Bowker's *Complete Video Directory, The Software Encyclopedia, Words on Tape*, etc.

TIP: Having an ISBN for each title is a good thing. But the best thing is to get it fully

registered with the R.R. Bowker "gods" so that you are ensured that your titles are in the *Books in Print* database.

Once you know the ISBN for your book, return to the Bowker website and register your title with its unique ISBN. Now, your ISBN will be linked with the appropriate title in Books in Print, the database that Bowker shares with retail book buyers.

Get Your LCCN Before You Publish Your Book

IF YOU WANT LIBRARIES to carry your book, you want an LCCN, which is good for all forms of your book (print, "e", audio). Apply for your Library of Congress Control Number (LCCN) after you have your ISBN number. There is no cost.

Go to:
https://locexternal.servicenowservices.com/auth

This is the Author-Self-Publishing portal to start the process to get the PCN, the Preassigned Control Number that will automatically convert to the LCCN. On your book's copyright page, identify it as the LCCN.

TIP: Stay on top of the LCCN process.
Too many authors think that because they applied for it in the first step, that's all they need to do. Get the data in, then look for the email acknowledging you exist and grants you permission to continue with your application. Then complete the rest of the info requested.

FRONT MATTER AHAs ...

Endorsements can be added before your Title page—a shout out for you and your book from your fans.

Copyright Page Musts: what you include, and don't include on your copyright page is revealing to book buyers. For libraries, the lack of specific data can be a book purchase deal breaker!

Your ISBNs, LCCN and CIP data are all posted on your copyright page.

The Copyright Year that is used is usually the current year you publish in. BUT, if it's between September and December, use the next year's. Why? It gives your book a longer "new" life.

Disclaimers: some books need a disclaimer of some sort—typically, it's found on the copyright page.

Publisher info: make sure you include publisher name and contact information.

Of the 18 books I published with New York traditional publishers, there were only two that I liked—that I was proud of. Some were so bad, I would apologize to my audiences from the stage when I spoke to groups. You don't want to be in that spot. A cover and interior designer should create a design that hooks the reader. Your designer should deliver a layout that is engaging, easy on the eyes, has some interest to the reader— callouts, white space, subtitles, chapter lead-ins, graphics, etc.

Not Using the Right Cover and Interior Designers

COVERS ARE THE BARKER to the reader and buyer. Your book shouldn't look like it was self-published, ever. Covers are a critical investment in the presentation of your book—not just the front, but the back. Where the front is designed to say what the book is about and conveys, "Pick me up now," it's the **back cover** that should get them to fall in.

Covers get Buyers to spend more time on the back, anywhere from 15 to 30 seconds. Headlines shouldn't be a repeat of the book title—this is your second sell. For nonfiction, are there three to five bullet points that are designed to hook the reader with "That's me, that's me," as they read through them?

A paragraph or two about the book and they should be sold, period. Don't get stuck on a bunch of endorsements—unless they are knock-your-socks-off comments and/or a major voice in your genre that your buyer, your crowd, will connect with, you probably don't need them. Always think benefit and value to the reader.

TIP: If there are more books in you that are related to the topic, think series and start your branding—with your image, logo, phrases, colors, title and your name.

39

Don't Expect a Book Designer to Read Your Book

HERE'S A SECRET MOST authors don't know: book designers do not read your book. Too many authors think they do and that they will catch boo-boos.

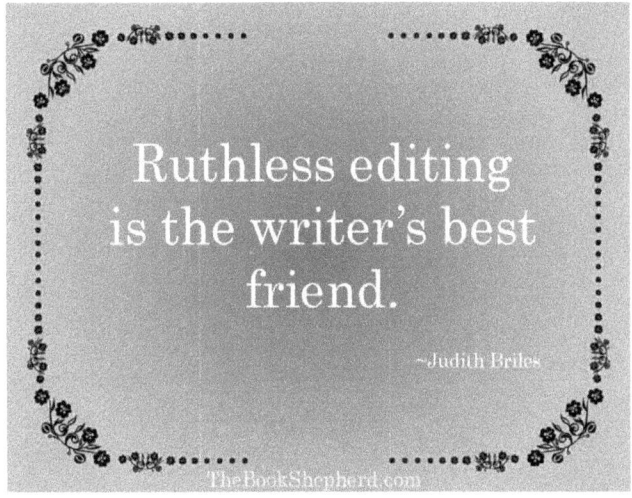

In fact, authors think it's part of the designer's tasks. Yes, sometimes something catches his or her eye ... but never expect a designer to be a proofer. It's not his or her job! The designer assumes what you forwarded is what you intended to have layed out—designed.

TIP: Remember: you are the reader for any final "catches" before your book is shipped off for printing.

40

Book Cover Designing Is Not a DIY Project

ON THE COVER, YOUR book should "shout" what it is about for nonfiction. For fiction, it should offer a hint, creating intrigue to bring the buyer in. Either says, "Pick me up; take me home." Having a cover designer who gets the book and has expertise in what sells and what doesn't along with what New York is displaying puts your book in a "competitive place." And your cover should be about branding for you and your expertise.

Whatever is on front has got anywhere from three to seven seconds to grab your reader.

On the back, deep magic needs to happen. Your reader has turned the book over. What's the headline? Now your marketing hooks come into play. Again, the cover designer knows tricks of the trade to make your key points—those ahas—pop and gather more attention. This is your major selling spot—anywhere from 15 to 30 seconds is spent on the back cover. It's your pitch—use bullets, shades of color to have a key quote or endorsement stand out. Your book has a beginning, a middle and an end: cover, content, back cover. I have never seen a DIY back cover that I could say, "This is awesome." Most are mediocre at best.

TIP: A book cover is an investment. Yes, a few books have done well with the brown paper bag, no thought in them approach—but just a few. With the millions of books being produced, wouldn't you rather have your cover knock it out of the park?

Your Book Back Cover Needs a Headline

A HUGE BLUNDER THAT DIY authors/publishers and traditional publishers make in back cover creation is the failure to create a headline to pull the reader in. Don't repeat the title of your book. Write something that is compelling and gripping. There's a reason why magazines, newspapers and the tabloids have special people who just create headlines. It's your book: shout-out.

TIP: Your back cover is priceless book real estate. Make sure the headline is big, bold and a grabber. Does it have emotional appeal? Does it identify a pain that your book is going to solve? Does it have some aha, salty or juicy—that the reader will be salivating to know what's on the inside?

ARE STABOTEURS™ IN YOUR MIDST?

- Are there bullies in your workplace?
- Do you have to deal with Pit Bulls with lipstick?
- Has anyone intentionally undermined you?
- Does your workplace keep the disrupters?
- Have you ever thought about quitting?

Every workplace has them—the pit bulls that hide behind lipstick and designer clothes; snakes who flick their abrasive tongues and voice at any and all; the scorpions who sting with a slap of their heavy backhand; the skunks that seem innocent until you get in their space; and the slugs ... those who are "just there" ... barely.

Stabotage!™ *How to Deal with the Pit Bulls, Skunks, Snakes, Scorpions & Slugs in the Health Care Workplace* reveals how to deal with the bad girls and boys that inhabit every environment ... be it one you get paid to be in or one you volunteer your time for.

Workplace pioneer Dr. Judith Briles has included her revised *CarefrontingScript*™ dialogue, the latest in communication techniques in dealing with conflict and toxic behavior, and the ins and outs of determining a workplaces true culture.

"I resigned from nursing three years ago. I couldn't take the attacks and abusive behavior any longer. Management did nothing. Their blindness caused a lot of good nurses to leave."
—SURVEY RESPONDENT #82

Business / Healthcare / Management / Nursing

$29.00
ISBN 978-1-885331-30-4

MileHigh Press

COVER DESIGN Rebeca Finkel, F + P Graphic Design
ILLUSTRATION Shannon Parish

BEFORE You Jump Into Design, Make Sure To Vet Your Prospective Book Designers!

What are their experiences in book production?

- This isn't the time for you to work with a designer newbie—you want someone who has years of experience. Your designer-to-be should have knowledge of book graphic design and software including *PhotoShop, InDesign, QuarkXpress* and *Illustrator.* Hands-on experience in the publishing industry is a must have. Otherwise, pass.

    - Get examples of their work. If they are in the business, their websites should be peppered with a variety of examples. If you meet in person, ask to see a variety of finished books they have created.

- Do they specialize in a specific genre? Most likely you don't want someone who is superb in horror to be working on your business book. There are twists and turns to fiction that just don't fit for nonfiction.

- Get references from other authors whose books the designers have done. Always ask, "Would you work with this designer again?"

- Up front, ask about costs. Some have flat fees; some, flexibility; some have a max number of re-dos allowed; some do both interior and cover design and discount when there is a combo. Know cost structuring in the beginning, including possible add-on costs.

- Contracts and agreements vary. Include deadlines, extra charges for changes, how payment(s) are made, if it's work-for-hire, who owns the rights, who owns the files, and that the designer will work with the selected printer in uploading files. Not all designers work with contracts. Expect to pay a deposit of 50 percent when the book layout is sent to you.

TIP: You want to work with a designer who is "current." Many have years of experience, but doing the same interiors and types of covers over and over. You want to work with one who is tuned into what is being produced by NY publishers. You may be self- or indie publishing, yet you want your book to look and feel like it rolled out of a traditional publisher.

Get Your Cover Design Completed First

THE EARLIER, THE BETTER, for your book project. Why? It creates the "face" for what you are doing and a "push" to keep moving forward. You add it to your website; to your signature on all emails that are sent out; share ongoing updates via your social media channels; and you can even create an Amazon.com/Advantage account and put it up for pre-sales.

TIP: Think of your book cover as part of your pre-launch and your pre-marketing. Once you have your cover (even if you tweak it a bit), it becomes a focal point to keep you going.

44

Avoid the DIY Look for Your Book Cover

MOST DIY BOOKS LOOK like DIY projects. Love your book; get a cover designer who does covers as a profession. You don't have to spend a fortune to get a great design.

In deciding on a style or type of cover—get to a brick and mortar bookstore. First, go to the section where your book would be placed if sold in the store. Look at every book that is competitive with yours. What covers pop? What do you like? What do you not like? Now, head to the front of the store. Walk around the "new" book section. What pops out? Colors? Fonts? Styles? You are doing an analysis of what you like and don't like. These are the current covers NY is pushing out. Eyeballs expect your cover to compete in style.

TIP: Your cover is your shout-out. If it doesn't say, "Come to me ... pick me up," it's not doing its job.

Does Your Back Cover Have the Blues?

YOUR BACK COVER IS the "real estate" where your pitch as to why the buyer needs your book. It should be pitch-perfect. Is it?

Start with a snappy, sassy, salty headline. A grabber—one that gets the eyeballs to stop, think "Tell me more," "OMG, this is for me." "Yes!"

Next, write a snappy description of your book and put it at the TOP of the back cover. It's your lead after the headline.

Readers shopping for books follow an age-old browsing routine. They check out the title, then flip the book over and look at the top of the back cover for a description of what's inside. Self-publishers seem bent on frustrating these potential buyers. They often leave this description off the book altogether, write it in convoluted prose or bury it at the bottom of the back cover.

Stop. Your copy needs to pull readers in. If it's nonfiction, concise short sentences on keypoints within; how the book will ease their pain or provide a solution. For fiction, study how book reviewers literally "rope" in readers with just one sentence—get a copy of the Sunday *New York Times Book Review* section. It's excellent as a guide—then add a paragraph or two that is snappy, sassy and salty. Welcome to marketing.

TIP: Write a crisp, enticing summary of your book and don't make readers break a sweat hunting for it. Use bullet points; make sure the cover designer uses design and graphic techniques that will highlight a key phrase, endorsement.

Cover & Interior Design 129

inspiration | memoir | self-help | grief

Does your life feel that it's too long, too hard, and not fair?

Have you experienced hurt, betrayal, fear, failure, critical illness, tragedy, or loss of a loved one? Have you asked or thought: "Why?" or lamented, "If only ..." or "Why did this happen to me ... to us?" If yes, **When God Says NO** is written for you.

Broke and broken when two of her children died, multi-award-winning author Judith Briles had to start over ... one step, one breath, one heartbeat at a time as she wove through her a life path littered with NO. Within her inspirational memoir, she reminds YOU that you are not alone when bad times surface. They will ... they do ...

My life became 50 shades of purple!

Despite the numerous setbacks in Judith's life, or rather, because of them, she found the tools to help her overcome any obstacle. Resilience became part of her DNA.

Get ready to embrace the joy of living, even when tragedy is in your midst. **When God Says NO** will change how you think; how you act; and your life.

Judith Briles is a speaker and author of 37 books. Known as The Book Shepherd to thousands, she works with authors, coaching them with practical publishing guidance. Calling Colorado her home base and working with clients world-wide, she marvels at the human spirit in its quest to survive and thrive.

www.TheBookShepherd.com

$20

ISBN: 978-1885331-83-0

9 781885 331830

The printing of books has dramatically evolved. Your book consultant and book designer will have recommendations for printers to use depending on your needs. Usually, there is a higher level of direct customer communication/service with offset printers than the digital printers who primarily communicate via online methods.

If you are a DIYer, request samples or books printed that would be similar to yours. If you need a lot of hand-holding, printing could be a stresser.

Printing Panache

There is printing and then there's printing. Contrary to the belief of many, print books do outsell eBooks in 90 percent of all genres. Understanding when POD (print on demand) versus an offset run is the better way to produce your book should be in your quiver of knowledge. Should you print a few books or many? Do you have color throughout or just on the cover? What kind of binding is best? What about add-ons: flaps, embossing, foil stamping, etc.? Each book has uniqueness, so does a printer. One that rocks with children's books may not be a fit for your fantasy series.

Not Engaging the Right Printer

THE PRINTERS THAT I use know the types of books I work with. Some printers are a better fit for a specific genre than others. They know how I want books to look, feel; they know the print runs I normally will request in a bid.

It's so easy to get in bed with the wrong one. Trust me here. When I did my first book under the umbrella of Mile High Press, I knew zip—and I mean it. After a dozen plus books with the traditional New York publisher, I was a "kept author." All I had to do was turn over my completed manuscript; respond to the editor questions and needs; and TaDah ... within 18 months, my book was in hand and in bookstores. Printers? Not even in my thinking sphere. New York took care of the book, the publicity *and* me.

> **But then, I was clueless—like so many authors first starting out on their own.**

Yes, I got that I needed a great cover (I had my share of OMG ... what was the publisher thinking?) and I knew that I need to find someone who designed the interiors of books. Those I found. But printers ... I mean, printing is printing. Right? Nope, I was so wrong.

That first book, a 2,000 print run was done by a local company referred to me that had no business bidding on a 2,000 print run. It was a company that was a short-run, POD operation. I hadn't heard of POD and didn't know what it meant. But then, I was clueless—like so many authors first starting out on their own. Short run ... what was that? Little did I know that the book I created cost me almost double what an offset run would cost. And let me lay my cards on the table. I didn't even know what an offset printer was, much less where and why I should get one.

The relationships that I have (and open up to my authors) are like the ones that a banker used to have with his depositors in the old days, pre-ATM and online banking.

Our printers know me and the books of the authors I refer to them. Does yours? In your quest for a printer:

- ✔ Get multiple bids. Ask for 500, 1,000, 1,500, 2,000 copies. Unless you have pre-sales that scream to get thousands in print immediately, stay with under 3,000. You will note that there is a true price break once you go above 1,000. Make sure you ask what a reprint run would be.

- ✔ Make sure that they are true book printers. There's a huge difference between laying out brochures and laying out books.

- ✔ Understand that color costs more. If you are using interior color, other than for your back and front cover, make sure you work with a printer who does color. Include both domestic and foreign printers in the bid process.

✔ Ask for references and samples of books that would be similar to yours and your specs.

If you are doing a short run or POD, meaning less than 500 copies (it could be just one!), get bids as well. Quality is critical—with emphasis on print as well as cutting of pages/cover. Ingram Spark has a full range of print/production services for the self-publisher in the POD realm. Amazon's CreateSpace is another option.

TIP: Today, there are less than 30 full book printers/manufacturers in North America. That number shrinks each year. Phil Knight, general manager of Color House Graphics, sees too often poorly designed books. His advice, "Talk to your printer early in the game—he can often suggest cost-saving options. Do it by hiring a professional to prepare your files. A good designer is worth his or her weight in gold—nothing hurts my heart more than hearing someone say, 'My friend from church has a nephew that knows computers' when I ask them who is helping them prepare files."

Your printer is a critical part of your team ... a major stepping stone to book completion. Your designer, book consultant or me as The Book Shepherd will make recommendations.

I even get the bids for my clients from multiple printers who I think will be the right fit for the book. Companies like Color House Graphics, Total House Printing, Friesens and Sheridan Books are on my targeted list to reach out to for consistent quality, pricing and customer service in the printing of books.

Avoid the Nightmare on Printing Street

DON'T BE A DIYER. One of the biggest mistakes, per Tim Hewitt with Friesens, is that too many in the self-publishing mode don't understand book design. Their typefaces look cluttered, the wrong typeface is used, and they don't understand the nuances of the trim area. He cautions authors to remember that manufacturing books is still a craft produced by humans using machines and there are variations in materials and equipment throughout the process.

Consider folding thousands of 48" wide sheets down to 6" wide and binding hundreds of pages together at home and see if you could possibly come within 1/16", ever. Even a variation of

1/32", or the width of a few strands of hair, will be visible to the human eye if these design elements are too close to the edge.

TIP: Do yourself, your printer and your customer a favor and leave good margins. White space is pleasing to the eye and is a mark of professional design whether you design it yourself or pay a designer.

Never Settle for Just One Print Bid

THE SAVVY AUTHOR/PUBLISHER gets at least three bids for printing a given book. If you are doing a POD format, not all print-on-demand vendors charge the same. Get multiple bids per copy here as well.

If you haven't seen the physical quality of the books by the print company, ask for them. Specifically, request a few samples that are in your genre. Ask for paper samples as well.

Always ask a printer if they have a specialty in printing, i.e. some printers do color best; others, high detailed map resolution. The range is huge.

TIP: Some of the best "print deals" pop up in January and February. Most printers aren't as busy during this time period and prices may be reduced.

49

POD May Be the Wrong Choice for Printing

MANY AUTHORS EXCLUSIVELY OPT for the POD option of manufacturing their books. It may be a mistake. POD can be ideal for creating advanced reader copies (ARC) for a test of potential readership; even a book that has had a good run and an author just wants to keep it available for buyers, yet not invest moneys in a full print run. It's also ideal for authors who can't afford a full print run.

The quality of POD has increased significantly since inception. For self-publishers, the two majors they will come across will be Amazon's KDP and IngramSpark. KDP has now surpassed IngramSpark in quality and customer service. The plus for IngramSpark is that bookstores can easily order books for instore events.

Hard cover books on POD: don't. It's costly and you may lose money per book in retail sales.

If you are planning on selling lots of books; putting an aggressive marketing campaign in play; hiring a publicity team to support your marketing efforts; creating special sales opportunities through speaking engagements; or desire a book in the landscape format, you need to move to offset printing pronto. Your cost per unit could be half (or more) of a POD cost, and the quality of the printing is superior.

TIP: Do the math. If you are selling books regularly; if you are speaking on your expertise; if groups are ordering your books by the dozens, start crunching numbers. Yes, you could have books in your garage or have minor warehousing costs ... but the net return to you will be far greater than the cost.

Which way to the warehouse?

Print Media Does Count!

Did you know that *USA Today* is the #1 paper that producers quickly look at to seed ideas and look at daily (even a number of times during the day)? Did you know that *USA Today* is the #1 paper that if you are featured in, could just be the "ticket" to get you the branding as an expert in your field?

If there is anything in your topic area, you can bet your local media has seen it too. Pick up the phone and pitch YOU to the News division of your local TV or radio station and ask them which program/host would cover your expertise and then reach out to the producer. Link YOU to the *USA Today* article. With the mobile world, don't make the mistake that it's only a stagnant daily paper. Reading it via the Internet allows for updates to be posted throughout the day.

TIP: *USA Today* is routinely taken by every major media outlet. Read it. The *USA Today* app is free. Make it a habit to peruse it daily to see if there is any breaking news that you can "news jack" and connect to you or your book.

Some of the best tutorials on
eBook creation and marketing strategies
can be found on the *Smashwords.com*
website. The essential guides:
The Secrets to eBook Publishing Success,
Smashwords Book Maketing Guide
and *Smashwords Style Guide*
are yours to download
free via the site.

eBook Ahas

If you have a print book, you want an eBook as well. And, if you have an eBook, you want a printed version available. Knowing which format the different eBook distributors require is essential; understanding how to use coupons along with free and promo days is key to marketing success; bundling your print and "e" version may increase your sales; and making sure that your "e" layout is done by someone who has the skills to make it look good should be at the top of your list.

Publishing an eBook with Errors Will Land Authors with an Amazon Warning and Possible Slap Down

AMAZON HAS BEEN THE self- and indie publisher's best friend. If you've got a book, Amazon will be a primary portal to sell it. Amazon also sells 70 percent of eBooks. Because of the ease of getting on Amazon, there are plenty of crappy books available.

In 2016, Amazon announced that it would slap warning labels on poorly edited books that include spelling typos and are identified under *Kindle Quality Reports*. Books that have formatting errors will be noted as well. Not knowing this and not dealing with it can easily cripple your eBook. There are two phases of the warning system. If your eBook contains a few spelling errors, a simple warning message will appear on the details page of your title. It offers a warning to the reader: Item Under Review ... or book buyer beware: there are some issues with the book. If there are bad formatting issues, and Amazon labels it as unreadable, your eBook will be suspended for purchase until it's fixed.

You don't want this warning label on your Title page, a warning that suspends your eBook from any sales via Amazon:

 Item Under Review

This book is currently unavailable because there are significant quality issues with the source file supplied by the publisher.

This publisher has been notified and we will make the book available as soon as we receive a corrected file. As always, we value customer feedback.

Amazon's positioning has been generated from the massive complaints from buyers who buy a book and then regret it. Many eBook sales come from impulse buys fueled by the low price point of most eBooks.

Unfortunately, some of those warnings are generated from the sci-fi and fantasy arena that contain odd names and spellings—in some cases like a new language. To counter the robots from the get-go, get back to your book and add a lexicon at the beginning that provides the "new vocabulary." This should ensure that your eBook is not thrown under the bus because of misspellings. If you do get tagged and Amazon notifies you, all you need to do is point to the opening pages where the new words and vocabulary are disclosed.

If yours has the British spelling of words, i.e. color/colour – favor/favour – honor/honour, just be consistent throughout. Don't mix them up with the American English spelling.
You will have ample warning. Amazon has notified many authors in the past two years of page issues and has allowed sufficient time to make the fixes. It looks something like this:

Issue: Typo. Details: "captial" should be "capital". Location: 611.

Issue: Typo. Details: "childern" should be "children". Location: 1095.

Issue: Typo. Details: "dictionry" should be "dictionary". Location: 800.

Issue: Typo. Details: "dispite" should be "despite". Location: 246.

Issue: Typo. Details: "dispite" should be "despite". Location: 303.

Issue: Typo. Details: "distrubution" should be "distribution". Location: 504.

Issue: Typo. Details: "formatrs" should be "formats". Location: 504.

Issue: Typo. Details: "has a increased" should be "has an increased\n ". Location 179.

In the past, Amazon has privately contacted authors/publishers of errors. No more; it now goes public. You don't want the slap down.

TIP: What should you do now? Read your eBook. Note any typos and formatting errors. Fix them by uploading a new copy. Normally, it takes two full days for Amazon to verify that your copy is clean. If you do receive a Kindle Quality Report warning. Fix whatever is noted and reload the new version. Amazon will then notify all previous buyers of the eBook that it's been updated and the warning label comes off.

Is Your eBook Format a Mess? Is It Ugly?

TOO MANY TEND TO think that formatting is something that doesn't need any time put into it. They think it's a DIY project. For eBooks, this couldn't be further from the truth. In general, eBooks are complicated; but in most cases, they are not. And that's where you can be seduced. Errors in formatting are common, even when the pros produce the eBook. That's why it has to be re-read once formatted. The DIYers believe that their PDF or Word document program will automatically format correctly. The answer is absolutely not.

Your eBook will turn ugly and be filled with glitches; ugly books create grouchy readers. This makes books appear unprofessional and often will end with poor reviews and returns.

TIP: Designer of eBooks, Nick Taylor, of *LightAndSoundGraphics.com*, advises: Take your time, do things right, and never forget the seven p's: perfect, prior, planning, prevents, piss, poor, products/performance.

Be sure your eBook designer is format savvy. However, as the author, you need to read the complete eBook to be positive no problems exist, including formatting.

Make Sure Your eBook Is in the Correct Format And Distribution Outlet

YES, AMAZON HAS ONE way, B&N another, iBook another. Don't think that one size fits all. And don't rely on having your eBook in a PDF format. A PDF format does not work well. It is a fixed layout and Amazon KDP, Barnes & Noble Nook, etc., use a "reflowable" format designed to display on screens that differ in size, width, etc. It's common for the reader to change font style and size of text at his or her whim—your fixed PDF won't allow it.

Make sure you discover *Smashwords.com* pronto (Amazon isn't the only game in author town and KDP Select may not be the ideal choice.)—dedicated to the indie world of eBooks, it's fast and free to set up. There are excellent tutorials on its website, and your eBooks are distributed to major retailers. Authors and publishers have complete control over the sampling, pricing and marketing of their written works. It's ideal for publishing novels, short fiction, poetry, personal memoirs, monographs, nonfiction, research reports, essays, or other written forms that haven't even been invented yet. The ability to tap into codes and coupons for "freebies"—think endorsements and reviews—for your eBook is an added perk.

If you choose the Amazon KDP Select option, you open the exclusiveness window: your eBook cannot be sold on any other platform during the 90 day commitment. You do pick up a special promo option: five days to offer your book for free. The regular KDP allows you to sell your eBook anywhere.

TIP: On *Smashwords.com*, there is a boatload of freebies for the DIYer—download them for your own reference library. Subscribe to its blog. CEO Mark Coker is visible and offers ongoing tidbits of cutting edge changes in

eBook land (including the pros and cons and is fearless in commenting on items, services and companies that he thinks are bad news for authors).

Invest in having your book converted to the appropriate format for eBooks (.mobi for Amazon Kindle; .ePub for Nook and the other platforms). There are a variety of services that convert your final PDF book into eBook language for just a few hundred dollars. Yes, you can do it yourself—but consider your time. Unless you are adept at conversion or it's a fun thing for you to do, use your time to promote and market your book.

Amazon has two eBook services: KDP and KDP Select. It makes sense to have your eBook posted on KDP—you should. KDP Select needs to be looked at closely—participating on it requires exclusivity. Pulling your book off of other eBook portals, i.e. Kobo, Nook, iBook, Smashwords, etc., may cost you sales.

Payments from each platform varies. Make sure you verify percentage payouts from the ones you are posted on. Don't overprice or underprice yours. Genres have "sweet spots" in pricing. Pricing an eBook at $11.95 and earning a 35 percent royalty pays $4.18 per book. If it had been priced lower at $9.99, the payout would be $6.99!

Without social media and the Internet, your book marketing efforts will most likely spiral into oblivion. Social Media is the portal to book marketing today. Knowing where your ideal buyer hangs out; creating the profile that shouts who you are; using the right key words and phrases (and yes, use hashtags); connecting with and following top influencers and bloggers will skyrocket your success.

Get Started Early and Engage Often via Social Media to Market Your Book

YES, YOU WILL MOST likely do some publicity and PR. But, both have taken a back seat in the book buzz world to social media—primarily, *Twitter, Facebook, YouTube, Instagram, Pinterest* and *LinkedIn*. If your book is for the YA crowd, definitely add TikTok and Instagram as key platforms to use.

Most likely you will need to create a *Facebook* page along with a Business page (and do all your posting about your book, its ahas and tips—anything—on the "book" or your "expertise" Fan page). Keep your personal page personal.

If your book is nonfiction, especially for business books or if you want to attract the media, Twitter is a must have tool.

Facebook is a never ending evolution. If your crowd is on Facebook, and most likely it is—get there too. One of the big mistakes authors make is that they mix up their "personal" page with their "author/book" news. Don't. Separate your political and any other views that could generate a negative opinion about you to potential Fans. And start a *Facebook Group* around your expertise for nonfiction. For fiction, it could be around a series, a genre, a location, and how about you? If you are creating SuperFans, they will be looking for you. Join my Facebook group recently created: Publishing with The Book Shepherd at:
https://facebook.com/groups/BookPublishingHelp

Get involved with groups on *LinkedIn*. In fact, for nonfiction authors, creating your own LinkedIn Group roots you in as a "go-to" authority and expert. Start discussions. You will have to moderate, but over time the group starts building on its own. For authors and anyone interested in publishing, I would encourage all of you to join the **Author YOU** group.

Pinterest is huge for the visual crowd. For cookbooks, it's a must have. If your book solves problems, you can easily create "Boards" with aha tips (I use BookBrush and Canva to make mine). Quotes by you or others can be generated in a Board; Cheat Sheets; Favorite Books; Awesome Beaches; Amazing Road Trips ... you get the idea. Have fun with this one.

Videos are hot and so is *YouTube*; create your own channel. Post on YouTube first, then cross post to your social media sites using its link. *Google* owns *YouTube*, the combo is huge. Don't ignore them.

One of the huge mistakes authors repeatedly make is to delay their social media strategies. The sooner you get this started, the better. If you are planning on doing any type of media with your book, don't be surprised when you are asked by a producer of a show, "How many Twitter followers or Facebook friends do you have?" You see, they expect you to do shout-outs about your appearance to promote it and the show. If you are a minor "player," you may not get a role. It's that simple.

TIP: Social media is all about finding your crowd, community, or "tribe" and communicating with it on an ongoing basis. Get started now.

55

Not Using Ninja Strategies to Push Your Social Media Out

SOMETIMES, AUTHORS MIX UP their priorities. Maybe they think they can "do it all" … stop it. When it comes to social media, you need a management system in place to schedule your posts; to follow comments; to make comments; to access what is happening in your "feeds." No, you cannot do it all. You are entering a chess board of options. Get help.

Social media tool options—you'll have many decisions to make: Which tool should you start with? Should you use specialized or multi-purpose tools? What features distinguish basic from intermediate to advanced and when should you upgrade from "free" to "fee" in a monthly cost?

If you can't define who your book is for, it's really for nobody. Social media is your town hall … it targets "who" your buyers are; it identifies potential SuperFans. Too often, authors make the mistake of thinking their books will appeal to almost "anyone" or "everyone." They're in for a rude awakening. Now, more than ever, the vast amount of self-published books in the marketplace makes it ESSENTIAL that you define your target market (not to mention your self-published book). That's the best way to find your niche, make it easy for them to find you, make them notice your book, and encourage them to recommend it to others. Your social media channels ease the way.

Social media tools make reaching social media marketing goals possible—in fact, stunningly successful. Whether you're an author with one book or with many, it's nearly impossible to manage a social media marketing program without using third party tools.

TIP: The first step is to know your market and what platforms it contains. Next, embrace one of the social media management systems to funnel all your postings through. You will

discover that you will whack off hours of time each day. And that's a happy dance for authors.

Find a system that works for you. *Hootsuite, Buffer, Sprout Social, Edgar, Post Planner, Sendible* and *AgoraPulse* are some of the top tools to use. Pick ONE … you aren't going to use them all. Some of my clients love Edgar, others Buffer. For me, I started with Hootsuite. It's what I know and it works for my postings. Explore them and then hone in on the one that "feels right" for you. Many have free 30 day trials; many have a free use if you have a limited number of social media channels you are posting to. For the fee ones, you will pay anywhere from $10 to $200 a month.

Hashtags Can Be Your Best Friend ... #!

DID YOU KNOW THAT reporters and writers routinely search hashtags to find experts for topics they are writing or reporting on? Did you know that topics that are being chatted on Twitter and Facebook are discovered quickly via their hashtag usage? If you are an expert and your book is about, or circles around, a trending hashtag, you should be in the game. Become a voice in the "trending topic" scene—whether it's for 10 minutes or 10 hours. If you are not using hashtags in your blogs, articles and your social media postings, you are making a major blunder in your searchability when posting on anything social media.

Create your own for special events, i.e., I could use #PublishingUnplugged for a workshop.

Or, I would use my name #JudithBriles. That way, insights and ahas can be easily followed on social media.

TIP: Discover what hashtags are used the most in your expertise and genre. Use them in your postings to increase your visibility with others who may not know of you or your social media platforms. Go to *Hashtag.org* **and explore.**

Hashtags are your friends!

Are Your Social Media Profiles Fresh or Stale?

MOST AUTHORS CREATE THEIR Profiles quickly, not really thinking of marketing/branding and leave them incomplete. Stop. Your Profiles are essential for search engine purposes as well as possible followers looking for savvy advice or someone that offers comments and tips in areas they are interested in.

At least twice a year, revisit all your Profiles.

- Are they current?
- Do they identify your expertise?
- Are you using key words or key word phrases so you are findable?
- Does your Profile clearly state what your expertise is? i.e.: *Dr. Judith Briles is a Book*

Publishing and Book Marketing Expert. It's who I am. What about you? Be specific and use "expert."

- How about your head shot ... is it you? Does it reflect some personality?

The *old* unwritten rules said to pick one picture and stick to it—no more, especially with Facebook. A new pic here just might generate plenty of comments and interaction.

TIP: When it comes to Profiles, don't simply do a copy/paste. Each social media platform has its own personality that includes the number of words or character counts—max yours. Take advantage of the space provided, increasing your searchability.

Where the Internet is the town hall of book marketing, you are the visionary and driver of it. Learning how to niche market so you don't waste your time, energy and money; knowing which magic mix of options you have available will bring in your crowd; getting your pitch to a prospective buyer of your book or services that generates a "Tell me more" response all are part of the focused effort that ninja book marketing authors use.

Start Selling Your Book Before It Is a Book

BOOK SALES AND DEALS can be done before a book comes out, or after it's in print. Make special offers. Take orders before it's printed. Pre-selling allows you to test the market response, your potential cover, and the price. Orders can be taken through your website (yes, you have one or will before your book comes out—a must-have on your Timeline) or create a flyer that you can distribute wherever you are. When people pre-pay, those funds should be used to offset your production costs.

If you think you are going to price your book at $20, offer it to early buyers at $20 and include shipping as a freebie. That's like getting a 25 to 30 percent discount if the buyer had to pay full retail plus shipping. Any resistance allows for tweaking—including a change in price. And, if there is no resistance to the $20, consider notching the price up a few bucks the next time you put your flyer out.

When I published *Money Smarts for Turbulent Times*, my pre-flyer had it pegged at $15. Quickly, I saw that I had priced it too low. Over a three month period, I had two price increases: to $20 then $25, finally settling at $25 when I went to print. For those who had committed at the lower price, it was honored. My pre-pub flyer was posted on my website and whenever/wherever I spoke, and routinely, I was successful in covering the cost of the first printing run with my pre-sales.

Pre-sell to groups that know you. If you are a speaker, distribute flyers everywhere you present; if you have an Internet following, tell your fans your news—you've got a book coming and because they are your fans or clients, they can order a copy at a special discount and receive it before others.

Your book may tie into a company or a product that would make it an ideal candidate for sponsorship or being used as a premium for a group. Sometimes it falls into your lap, other times, you need to pursue leads.

TIP: Pre-selling your book gives you instant feedback ... is the demand there? Do you need to adjust your price?

You may discover those who want to pre-view/review your book. Make sure you start gathering emails of all you come in contact with. Also carry mailing labels. Why? It's done—all you need to do is attach labels to your book boxes or padded envelopes for shipping. And the buyers are self-addressing it at the time of pre-purchase, meaning it's their handwriting—so they should be correct.

Preordering isn't exclusive to a printed book, don't forget your eBook version and if you know an audiobook will be created, take preorders as well. iBook allows preorders up to 12 months prior to publication where Barnes & Noble and Kobo allow up to 9 months. Amazon only allows up to 3 months in advance of your eBook availability.

Smashwords' Mark Coker has created several guides to rocking eBook preorder strategy that you can find on its site: *Smashwords.com*. Do a search for "preorders" and "assetless."

Creating and Offering Pre-Publication and Post-Publication Flyers

TIMING IS IMPORTANT. THINK about pre-selling six months prior to actually having book in hand. Give yourself a little flexibility—saying that a book will be shipped on February 1st might sound far off the previous October—it's really only three to four months away depending on which part of October you are talking about. Let's face it, things happen that could delay a book—be they rewrites, interior or exterior design, editing, printing. Or just maybe you've lagged a tad. A little breathing room helps. Instead of saying that your book will be available February 15th, it's better to say winter. That gives you a three month window. Spring doesn't start until much of March has passed. If you have settled on the price, offer your special at that price with the free shipping as the incentive. That's going to give the buyer a decent discount. Let the buyer pay by cash, check or credit card. Don't spend the money before printing. It's usually one of your bigger chunks to pay for and this is the ideal spot to direct prepayment moneys to.

Before you ship books out, create a form or flyer that is included with all book shipments about any of your other books and services. The buyer has your book in hand, and now has more information about services, products or other books that you offer. This makes your book fulfillment mailings another avenue for marketing.

TIP: As the Chief Marketing Officer (CMO), it's your job to get your book out there. Any time you can put something in someone's hands—flyers, postcards ... anything that says you and your book solve problems—that provides value and/or entertains. You hit a homerun.

Seek Out and Pitch Book Clubs

BOOK CLUBS DON'T PAY top dollar, but they buy books (at a deep discount), pay you quickly, and don't return them. There are general interest, lifestyle, special interest, and professional clubs.

Savvy authors seek out book clubs. Your local bookstores often are suppliers of books for them--do the ask. Libraries are excellent resources to identify them as are Meetup groups and churches. Of course, an online search. Start with Google. Do a search for "[your area name] book club" ... the results will most likely identify several in your area.

- *BookSpan.com*
- *OnlineBookCLub.org*

Don't forget companies. Don't be surprised to discover that departments within companies may have their own book clubs. If you are doing any consulting or speaking, just ask your contact. Last summer, I visited a friend at a Denver hospital. In just chatting with one of the nurses, I discovered that not only did the leadership team get together monthly to discuss a book ... but guess what? My book *Stabotage! How to Deal with the Pit Bulls, Skunks, Snakes, Scorpions and Slugs in the Health Care Workplace* was featured the previous month, meaning that 43 copies were bought for participants!

TIP: Many bookstores work with local book clubs. Identify who the contact person is at your local bookstore to determine if there are any clubs that might be a fit for your book and then reach out.

BONUS TIP: Include a Book Club Discussion page at the end of your book. Include questions, dilemmas and situations to generate conversation. Invite the club members to set up a Skype call with you. Make sure you include your contact information on the page.

61

Target Your Media/PR Marketing

IF THERE EVER WAS a giant sucking sound in publishing, this is the arena that usually gets the most votes. Mega thousands of dollars can be kissed off in the area of PR and publicity.

Most people, and certainly authors, would assume that if a program/plan was created, moneys committed to it, that there would be success—meaning books would be sold.

Not so with PR … it's a Maybe, Maybe Not world.

In PR and publicity, authors and publishers quickly learn that there are no guarantees. You may be scheduled to do a segment on a coveted program and get bumped at the last minute because of late breaking news i.e., Kim Kardashian joins convent). Yes, your info is more important ... but producers have quirks as to what "they" think is news worthy—and unfortunately, often "junk" rises to the top. Kim Kardashian, or whatever deep doo-doo the celebrity of the week is newsworthy of. And in, is now. You are expendable. You are "out."

Or some crises or tragedy hits. Anyone who had planned a media blitz when 9/11 hit did an instant vaporizing act. The same with the disappearance of the Malaysian Flight 370; a massive tornado strike that evaporates an entire town like the one that hit Joslin, Missouri; or the outrageousness of the 2016 GOP debates. You, or the person you hire to rep you, can pound the media circuit and pitch ... and get zero results. You can't compete with it.

This doesn't mean that you can't "hook" your book with an event if it's appropriate. What happens when the "unexpected" happens during an author tour?

Years ago, I was doing promotion for my book, *The Confidence Factor*. Scheduled to be on *The Morning Exchange*, the top-rated morning TV show in Cleveland, Ohio, at the time, a local tragedy occurred the night before. Graduation night, teens drinking and driving, there was an accident. Three of the "star" students died including the president of the class.

The city was waking up to this awful news; family and friends were mourning and I was scheduled to be bright and perky. Caramba! ... I'm supposed to be upbeat and inspirational— it was the wrong time and wrong fit for upbeat and perky.

As I listened to the news segment that preceded me, I turned to the host off-camera and said, "I know that I'm supposed to talk about my latest book here, but I have another one that would be more appropriate. It's called *When God Says NO* and opens upon the death of my 19-year-old son from an accident. Would it be OK if I lead with this instead of my new book?"

With sad and teary eyes, all he could do was nod his head "yes" and lead as the camera light flashed on. I'm introduced and took over saying what I said above and said, "With the show's permission, I would like to divert from my new book and talk from my heart." I restated what had happened with my son, how it affected family, friends and the community.

What happens when young people with huge futures ahead and suddenly, everything is yanked away? You see, I knew exactly the pain that was going on; I could feel it in that room. When Frank died, 10 of his friends were with him; they heard him slip and fall off a bridge. None of them should have been climbing on it; just doing kid stuff that kids do. The panic the kids felt as they scrambled to find him; the zombie-like actions that we observed and experienced as we worked with the kids; the news that took over our community on that fateful Labor Day weekend that was even aired over a thousand miles away on a radio show that a friend heard and the calls that followed.

I revealed how I was devastated when Frank died; his younger sister who was with him needed huge support; I was bombarded with the media; even his beloved dog lost all her hair. I did all I could for myself and my family to keep from drowning in sorrow. Yes, I spoke from my heart—I knew exactly what was circling around the families and city of Cleveland, Ohio, that horrendous morning.

As I shared, they listened, asking few questions; the crew was frozen as they watched and listened. What I didn't know was what was going on at the switchboard. Massive phone calls were coming in. The station was overwhelmed. *Viewers wanted to hear more—they needed to hear more.* The producers were telling the hosts that they were bumping the next two segments and segue to keep me there via their ear pieces. We went for three segments, two beyond what I had been scheduled for.

Leaving with thank yous and hugs all around, the head producer approached me and asked if I would be willing to come back in a few weeks and do another show around the theme of Overcoming Adversity—arranging all the transportation and accommodations. Of course, I would and did.

Upon my return, it was a huge welcome back, and yes, I was able to now lie back and mention *The Confidence Factor* ... one of the factors was dealing with adversity and failure. A full hour was dedicated to the topic and three other locals joined in—one psychologist, and the other two adults who had experienced sudden tragedy. You have to ask: Did your PR rep do a crummy job? Is there no interest in your topic? Is your information material, including media release or hook, mediocre? Is there major news that is bumping everything? What?

It is critical to be focused and targeted. PR and no-guarantees go hand-in-hand. The more that the author steps up to the plate to assist in the orchestrating of the campaign—even pitching it—the more success can come your way. And, it's important to understand that "traditional" media—such as pitching to national television or radio—may not be the right fit. And it's important to understand that you must be flexible.

Ask yourself:
- What does your crowd—your book buyer—watch or listen to?
- What are the media channels (print, TV, radio) in your community?
- What shows feature authors and books?
- What shows feature experts?
- What themes are carried on the "event"

calendar for your local newspaper?
- What are the freebie/throw-away news outlets in your region?
- What are the online news resources in your community?
- What Internet shows/podcasts would be a fit for your book?
- What are the groups that share the message of your book. How do they connect with their members?
- What is currently "hot" in the media and how can you tie your book into it?

TIP: *Ellen* and *Good Morning America* isn't for everyone. There are, though, thousands of other venues that are the perfect fit for your topic.

Use Your Books as Your Business Calling Card

A WELL-DONE BOOK that is presented to a new or old acquaintance could be the link that seals a deal. Books that are self-published shouldn't look like they are self-published—either inside or outside. With the massive resources available to anyone, cheap looking books and poorly written ones should go the way of the dinosaur.

TIP: Well-done doesn't mean over-done. Get professional editors and designers on your team for both the cover and interior. This way a book should never have to be apologized for or tossed in the trash.

Thinking Your Book Is for Everyone Is the Kiss of Death for Book Sales

THE MOST COMMON RESPONSE of an author when asked who his book is for is, "Everyone … everyone should have/read my book." Nonsense. No one's book is for everyone … if you will remember this one thing: *the more you niche yourself, the bigger your market can become*, you will be able to deep-dive into connecting, relating, interacting and knowing your true market.

TIP: Narrowing down who your ideal reader is keeps you focused in your writing and creates a homerun for any book marketing efforts, including social media outreach.

Ask for an Amazon Review Upfront

YOU NEED THEM … AND so do potential buyers. In this case, the more the merrier. You want a minimum of 25 on launch week. Your objective is to surpass 100. It takes work. Start now and continue. Don't be shy: you need them. Please go to Amazon and post one for this book as well.

TIP: Create a postcard or bookmark that has your cover on one side and info about you, the book and a "Help an Author Out" … the HAAO effect. Create a short URL to the lengthy Amazon URL. Do this by using a site like *Bit.ly* or *TinyUrl.com* and shorten … both will let you customize. For example, for my book, *The Crowdfunding Guide for Authors & Writers*, I created:

http://bit.ly/CrowdFundGuide

My buyers could easily remember it versus the breadth of characters and words that a typical Amazon URL creates.

Amazon's full link looks like this:
http://www.amazon.com/CrowdFunding-Guide-Authors-Writers/dp/1885331576/ref=sr_1_sc_1?ie=UTF8&qid=1457108640&sr=8-1-spell&keywords=the+crowdfundng+guide+for+authors.

The shortener is clearly better and memorable.

And for postcards, make sure you make it look like a "real" postcard with a mailing address space so that you can use them for marketing.

Your Book Isn't for Everyone ... Get Over Thinking It Is!

ONE OF THE MOST COMMON mistakes authors and writers let roll out of their mouths when asked "who" the book is for ... respond, "Everyone needs my book."

No they don't. Get real, who REALLY is your book for. Men? Women? Kids-what age? Singles? Marrieds? Partners? Who Knows? Addicts? Workers? Retirees? Travelers? Cooks? Diseases? Post College? High School Grads? Lovers of Horror? WHO? It's a long, long list out there.

TIP: The more you niche yourself, the bigger your market becomes. When you know WHO your market reader is, writing is easier and so is the marketing when the book is completed.

Create Your Tag Line That Supports Your Branding

FROM THE BEGINNING, AUTHORS need to know who they are and what they bring to their readers. You are an Expert ... create a tag line that expresses what you and your books do to benefit the reader/client/follower, with just a few words.

Mine is: *Creating Successful Authors with Practical Publishing Guidance.*

TIP: Once you have your Tag Line, incorporate it in all your social media profiles; get it under your name in the banner on the top of your website as well as the headers/banners on Facebook, Twitter and other social media pages.

Beware of the Word-of-Mouth Myth

BUZZED ABOUT FOR DECADES, authors love to believe that all they need is to get their book out there and with a few good reviews, the word of mouth power will flow. Stop—word-of-mouth can be an illusion.

You need to know where your readers are hanging out. Do they love brick and mortar bookstores? Are they primarily online (i.e. Amazon) buyers? Are they conference and workshop attendees who buy directly from the presenter? Are they review readers? Do they get all their reading ideas from book clubs? Where? Book clubs and bookstores are often joined at the hip. Contact your favorite bookstore and see if they will connect you with book clubs in the area. If you think your buyers are dedicated to the traditional bookstore, then befriend the store, the buyer, the event coordinator and see what avenues you have open to you to advertise your book and appear in the store. If your buyers are at conferences, get on the speaking circuit. If they buy via reviews, concentrate on building Amazon, Goodreads, Shelfari and certainly don't forget the print media. Those local weekly throw-aways could be gold. Submit a short article, even a review by someone else. It could easily be printed. Space has to be filled.

TIP: Word of mouth is possible, but there is lots of work behind the phenomenon to make it happen. The book buying world isn't coming to you until you go to it.

Savvy Authors Start Marketing Their Book Before It Is Published

MARKETING IS AN ONGOING endeavor for all authors—sometimes exciting but often overwhelming—and usually not even thought about until the book is written and ready to sell. Waiting until there is a "book in hand" is poor planning—impacting the journey. Most authors think the most time-intensive part is the writing and creation of the book. That's only 10 percent of the journey; the other 90 percent is marketing the book—ideally, from the get-go.

TIP: Marketing needs to become embedded in the author's DNA as soon as the book begins. Platform building; social media presence; and website development are all part of the infrastructure of author success.

Not Creating the Perfect 15-Second Pitch

WHEN SOMEONE ASKS YOU what your book is about, can you clearly and concisely say it in 15 seconds or less? Most authors fail miserably at this essential task. When his or her mouth opens, words flow ... and flow ... and flow. Sometimes, words can become an endless river. They ramble on about the background; why the book was written; who the characters are and what they do; how the book solves all the problems of the disease, the situation, the "you name it." The concept of being "concise" doesn't register in their response.

Around you are the voices of thousands of people competing for space in your buyers' and readers' heads. Learn how to get your voice, your expertise, and your book, heard above the clatter and racket of the book crowd.

You want your pitch to create one response from the listener: *Tell me more.* The listener may think it; he or she may say it. Your pitch needs to elicit it.

As you acquire the skills for pitching yourself and your book, you will discover that the results adapt to publicity and marketing, as well as the direct book buyer and anyone else who lands in your path.

TIP: Authors are notorious when it comes to talking about their books ... or trying to describe what their books are about. The savvy author knows how to *Pitch*, and hook the listener quickly and succinctly. The result? *"Tell me more about ..."* becomes the response. The author has thrown the lure out—the portal is now open to engage the potential reader/book buyer and reel him in.

Within your pitch, use one or more of these elements:
1. your words should create an instant visual;

2. your words need to be succinct;
3. your words can be quirky and fun;
4. your words can include something familiar;
5. your words can have a rhyme meter and rhythm to them;
6. your words can use alliteration.

    The result: you will sell books.

There are three magic words that all authors want to hear when pitching his or her book to a producer, reporter or a book buyer ... **TELL ME MORE!**

You get them when you are clear and concise with your message. Practice your Pitch. Memorize your Pitch.

Blogs can be your book's best friend—yours too. Be committed, consistent and add content that your followers want and in some cases, need. When you post a new one, let your followers on social media know it's there with a link. Don't forget to add images to each post and make sure that your blog is visible and easily accessed on your website.

Blogging Creates Fans ... Are You Doing It?

RAVING FANS, MEANING THE types that devour anything you offer, are created with high content and consistency.

- Where are you on the blogging scale?
- Is your blog posted on your website or is it a stand alone?
- How committed are you?
- Do you post once a week or more often?
- Do you offer a common theme within your expert area or are you all over the place?
- Do you use images within your blog?

Blogs can soar your expertise reputation, bringing you business and fans. Not having a blog is a huge mistake for authors and writers. They don't have to be long—varying them in length is fine. What they do need is consistency. Your readers can count on you to provide informative, entertaining, even challenging information on a consistent basis; content is rich. You provide info that supports your reader's journey, and enriches a topic area. And commitment—you post on a specific day each week (that doesn't mean you can't post more often).

TIP: If you decide that Tuesday is your blog post day, then every Tuesday you deliver. If a holiday such as Christmas is on Tuesday, you still have a new post. The content doesn't have to be religious (although you can choose to). What you post every Tuesday says to your followers that you are committed and constant. What content you deliver is up to you.

Discover sites like Hootsuite and Buffer that will allow you to post out to your followers when new blogs are up. If you are using a website platform, such as WordPress, you can easily create several and schedule them to be released over a period of time. That means you can go on vacation and no one will know … you have your "committed" hat on if your blog comes out on the day your fans expect it to—even if you are cruising to the Bahamas.

Are You Connected with Bloggers … the Portal to Book Reviews?

TODAY'S BLOGGERS ARE YOUR reviewers … and there are more than 150,000,000 blogs. Eyeballs are devouring information online. Your awareness level is in play every time you are online … and advertisers know it. Have you noticed the significant increase in ads being posted? Huge moneys are spent by companies that provide services and products. They have moved their money to the Internet.

Review copies should be sent to book bloggers and subject-matter-expert bloggers who focus on *your book's category*. If you aren't doing this, you are missing the review opportunity boat. For example, books on leadership should only go to blogs on leadership; cookbooks to blogs on cooking, recipes; sci-fi goes to the fantasy, future, sci-fi bloggers; etc.

There are bloggers, bloggers on subjects and book bloggers. All are valuable to you but the book bloggers are the best because they write about books and are book-category oriented. Few read and comment on anything else but their specific category topic.

The great majority of book bloggers are female and moms.

To find these kindred spirits, make a Google search for "book blogger directory." Now narrow it. If you have a book on overcoming depression, search for "depression and anxiety book blogger directory." You will be amazed at what you find.

You can also start with an existing network of book bloggers and book reviewers:

https://www.LibraryThing.com/ (general)
https://Goodreads.com (general)
https://SFBook.com/ (sci-fi and fantasy)
https://www.Bookpage.com/ (kids and general

Now, it's hunter and gatherer time: you need to discover bloggers' names, email addresses and other contact details.

Remember, these aren't just any bloggers; they are those that love books in your category (such as depression and anxiety). They are members of your growing tribe. They love the same subject you love and that you are an expert in.

Use an Excel spreadsheet to input your information that is gathered: contact details, names, emails, phone numbers, street addresses, blog names, etc. Using Excel allows your list to become "sortable." It is easy to add to and it's easy to pull off the postal and email addresses for individual and group mailings.

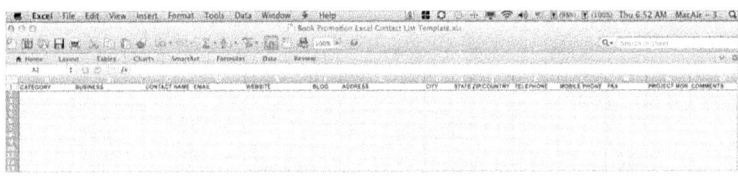

The columns may be labeled: category, business name, contact name, email, website, blog, address (as in street address), city, state, zip code/country, telephone, mobile phone, fax, project manager, and comments.

The category column is where you list whether it is a blog, forum, website, print magazine, etc. Avoid the general review categories. You want reviewers who are interested in your subject, which means their followers are interested in it—your potential book buyers. You will use this list to send review copies, news releases, and other announcements on your subject and book and will be used over and over again.

TIP: Bloggers can become your advertisers ... book bloggers ... the new book reviewers. Assembling your list will be increasingly valuable. You will discover people all around the world interested in your subject and

who would be interested in your book. Reviews and mentions sell books. Make up your list of bloggers now and start connecting. When you get reviewed, shout it out on your social media platforms and link to the reviewer's site. If the blogger hasn't posted the review on your Amazon page, ask them to (include the link so it's an easy copy/paste).

Publicity & PR

Opportunities abound when it comes to publicity for you and your book. Learning how to news jack trending stories when you can connect them with you and your book or expertise can cascade PR your way; knowing how to pitch to the media; using press releases and engaging the who, what, where, when and why leads to media awareness and dominance in your expertise field.

Your Book Isn't for Every TV/Radio Show and Media ... Get Over Thinking It!

ONE OF THE MOST common things new "authors" do is misdirect their publicity. They place in practice "BB Gun Marketing" versus a focused, narrow lane. Not doing *targeted* media/PR marketing when it comes to publicity exposure is the kiss of death. All media and PR coverage should be directed to avenues that have buyers for your book. Just because you love Dr. Phil or think Fox News is the cat's meow doesn't mean it's the right place to pitch your book.

TIP: Use list of top book buying cities (Seattle, San Francisco, New York, Denver, Minneapolis, Portland, etc.) to pitch to radio, TV and print

audiences. BUT, don't forget that there are oodles of smaller radio and TV stations that might have the perfect audience for you.

You are going to need a spread sheet of some sort; target a city or state and simply Google who the players are. Many of the emails are online and certainly phone numbers. Call and ask who the producers are, get their names spelled correctly, ask for emails and reach out. If TV, watch the shows you want to pitch to. At the end, pause on the credits and write down the producers' names. Any Media and PR that you do are basic sales ... sell the benefits of your book to the listeners, viewers, readers. And remember: *Rachel Ray, Kelly Clarkson, CNN, FoxNews,* or *Good Morning America* aren't for everyone.

Register with FREE Sites to Connect with Media for Publicity

IF YOU ARE POSITIONING yourself as an Expert (you are, aren't you?), make sure you are receiving eblasts from HARO (Help a Reporter Out). It's a free service that reporters and writers use to seek out experts and to find sources for their stories. Each day they send out three emails with lists of requests from reporters. Within the email are quick bullet point types of queries. If any address your expertise area, the contact info is there for you to reach out with your mini-pitch of who you are, what your expertise is, and how to contact you. Simple.

In just a few minutes you can scan the list to see if anyone is looking for an expert in your topic area. If not, delete it and continue with your "work."

TIP: Sign up at the HARO website:
   http://HelpAReporter.com
and don't hesitate if you see something that might fit your book or expertise. With HARO, it's the early responder that gets the reporter's worm.

Author Photos Should Be Created By a Pro

AUTHORS NEED PHOTOS, PLENTY of them. Nothing shouts "unprofessional" like a headshot taken in front of a wall inside or outside of your house. They come across as flat, which is what you don't want to do. A more casual head-shot/"action" shot allows your personality to shine through and works well in specific areas of your marketing: Author One-Sheets, Book One-Sheets, websites and social media profiles. Make sure you have a Media tab on your website and include a few there that can be used.

When is the last time you had a "photo shoot" by a professional photographer who "gets authors"? This is not a standard business headshot or something like a college grad photo (yet, most are). You want some casual; some in a surrounding that you love or are inspired by; some that show a sense of fun; how about a few outdoors? Authors have moved beyond the plain vanilla type of photo to one that is more reflective of their personality, their work, their play.

TIP: Invest in a professional headshot(s)— one that is more "formal" and one that is more "casual." Make sure you get the rights to use your photos in any manner you desire without having strings attached to how many times it can be used. When interviewing photographers, ask to see their portfolio samples of other authors and personalities they've done. Ideally, you want one price for

multiple shots that you can use over and over and the photographer puts all the finished images on a disc and/or sends them to you via email. Of course, you save them in a separate folder on your computer as well as on a backup flash drive.

Author and Book One-Sheets Are Necessities

THINK OF A ONE-SHEET as a "brag sheet" for the author or book.

For the *Author One-Sheet* ... include one or two images of you; a few great quotes or endorsement blurbs; content that states your expertise; use bullet points to bring attention to benefits you bring to the reader (or a coordinator or planner who is in charge of getting authors for book clubs and speaking); blurbs from key book reviews; your key book titles; contact information: phone, email, website, social media images. An *Author One-Sheet* is different from a *Speaker One-Sheet*. The latter will have an emphasis on speaking titles, topics, and testimonials from groups that say you are a rock star on the platform.

For a *Book One-Sheet*, include your cover and if you have "art" on the interior—the opening page of a chapter with images that deliver some type of variable to the line text—eye candy for the visual side; images of logos from any major media you have appeared on; blurbs from key book reviews; if the book is part of a series, mention other titles, sometimes include cover images (make sure the current book cover pops out over the others); if it has won awards or hit a bestseller status, mention or include images reflecting who the awarder is; bullet points of key points from the book for nonfiction (ID what pain—what solution—what benefit there is to the reader); for fiction—hook the reader with a creative lead-in (most likely pulled from back cover); contact information for author: phone, email, website, social media images.

TIP: One-Sheets are handy tools to have. Carry extras to give out at presentations or for general interest about you or your book. Create the PDF to post on your About the Author or About the Book tab on your website; also place it in your Media tab.

Outside of the written One-Sheet for Book and Author, create a one to two minute video version and load it on your website plus to your YouTube channel and pin it to your Pinterest site.

The gorilla of online book sales awaits you. Don't ignore the power of Amazon as your primary retail book distributor—for the majority of authors, it is. Yes, people go to brick and mortar bookstores and other online channels like BN.com to buy and libraries to borrow books as well. But for fast sales with a few clicks, Amazon is a "must have" for visibility and clickability. Ideally, have an Advantage account, Amazon's publisher window. Set up your Author Central account. Have an Amazon "buy" button link on your website along with one for your local bookstore of choice.

Amazon ... You Can Love It - Hate It ... But You Need to Use It!

WHEN YOU HAVE YOUR book cover, create an *Amazon.com* along with your *Author Central account* on Amazon. Set up your Author Central account at *AuthorCentral.Amazon.com.*

Note—you need to have at least one book for sale through Amazon in order to set up an Author Central account.

Start loading info about your book, along with any endorsements received (and about you within the Author Central account).This is another gateway to gather orders. Some of my clients have actually gathered more than 1,000 pre-orders from Amazon before their book was available.

Author Central is like a secret sauce. It's the single fastest way to get a "live" person from Amazon to talk to. If you have a critical question, a snafu of some sort, even wonder if you are in the right category, you are able to go to your Author Central account, click on the "Connect/Talk" or whatever they call the icon at the moment on your page. Within seconds, your phone rings and you get help. I'm amazed at the speed of the call and the helpfulness on the other end.

Summing Up: Your benefits of setting up an Author Central Account on Amazon include:

1. You can speak with a LIVE PERSON at Amazon! How long does it take to connect with someone—is five seconds fast enough?

2. A live person can do magic—help you with getting the "right" categories for your book listing; make sure you are in the right positioning if you are doing a best seller's push; get things fixed when they go missing from your account; get other books and offerings connected to your account that should be and aren't. Just ask; they will tell you what they can do and can't do.

3. It is free to set up an Author Central account as soon as you have your book listed on Amazon.

4. You have more "control" over the content you submit for your book description, including from the author, from the inside flap, from the back cover, etc.

5. You can add your blog feed to your Author Central Account.

6. You can connect your social media account to your Author Central Account.

7. You can upload videos and images to your Author Central Account. Great opportunity to share your book teaser video!

TIP: Most likely Amazon is going to be the biggest outlet, outside of you, for your book. Take advantage of it.

Reviews ... Ask and You Will Get!

AS AN AUTHOR, IT'S not the time to be shy. You want your buyers to post reviews. The two main ones would be *Amazon.com* and *Goodreads.com.*

Amazon has millions of buyers of books. They read reviews. The more reviews that you can get posted, the better. They count and tell the viral world that others are reading and liking your words.

Goodreads is a source that many librarians check out. They want to see what readers and consumers are saying about current books, especially in the self-published and independent published arenas.

TIP: Create a sign up page on a clipboard and carry it with you. Gather names for your blog at the same time. Now that you have a contact and email, you can reach out and send a reminder with the link to where you want reviews posted. Don't be surprised to have to repeat your request.

Make sure that you make a habit of going into Amazon and Goodreads and copy the Reviews that get posted. Use them on your website in a type of "people are talking" format, and make sure you create a "master" of them on your computer in a special folder.

Don't Work Exclusively with Amazon

WHY DO YOU ASK? Simply this: bookstores are not enamored to order a book through competitor Amazon if a customer comes in and requests it and Amazon via KDP is the only option.

TIP: If you are doing a POD format, make sure you have your book in both *KDP, BN.com* and *IngramSpark.com.* Bookstores have been ordering books from Ingram for decades—they trust it. Lightning Source prints all IngramSpark's books. Print quality and customer service are essential. As of 2022 KDP is winning in both categories. Being in Ingram's catalog yields great author/book power—bookstores and libraries for resale or use.

My recommendation: If you elect to do a POD printing, create a "short run" of less than 1,000 books with a traditional book printer, also known as a book manufacturer. Your cost will be less per unit (sometimes as much as 50%). At the same time, create a book marketing plan to speak and sell books onsite at events, fairs, book events. Welcome to the world of how to move and sell books.

Amazon Is Your Ally ... Set Up Accounts that Work for You

I KNOW, I KNOW—it discounts what it pays to you by 55 percent of your stated retail price. Get over it pronto. No matter how Amazon changes the price, you will still net 45 percent of the original retail price you posted on your book's content page. Amazon is the gorilla in book selling. And you are going to have to pay to get your books to its warehouse. Get over it. If you want your Amazon page to have a GREEN BUY button, plus be open for cross-promotions from the Amazon robots and gods, stop resisting. Amazon Advantage was created for publishers. OK, if you have produced a book and want to sell it. Yes, you *can* "net" more moneys if a book sells via Amazon's Market Place ... but you don't have all the bells and whistles that the Advantage book pages have—meaning that the odds are that your visibility and book sales will be less and book sales will be fewer.

TIP: Amazon is notorious for ordering one or two books at a time, meaning your shipping costs will be high to get books to its warehouse destination. Change it. Go to the Contact button once you are inside your Advantage account and send them an email requesting that a minimum of five books be ordered due to your warehouse's requirements; your ability to only get to the UPS, the post office—whatever—once a week; a special promotion that you have scheduled in two weeks to drive buyers to Amazon, etc. Within a day or two, you will get a response back—usually with an increased order amount. Your shipping cost per unit will drop dramatically. Now, move people to your page and sell books.

Don't leave bookstores off your book selling table. Yes, Amazon is a must have connection for anything online, but brick and mortar stores are alive and many are thriving. Indie Bound bookstores could be the perfect portal to support the IndieBound author. Ask your friends and local residents to connect with their local bookstore—get your book in their store to be able to buy directly and support bookstores. They will in turn support you.

80

Seek Out Independent Bookstores

BARNES & NOBLE IS THE gorilla of the major chain bookstores. Walmart and Target are also huge book sellers. It's great to get your book into a chain, but consider the independent bookstores—much easier to get your book on their shelves and create a signing. And local Indies are far more inclined to support the local author.

Here's a list of some of my favorites:
- Seattle WA - Elliott Bay Book Company
- Portland OR - Powell's City of Books
- Denver CO - BookBar, Bookies, Books Are Awesome, Tattered Cover
- San Francisco CA - City Lights Bookstore
- Menlo Park CA - Kepler's Books and Magazines
- New York NY - McNally Robinson Booksellers (also in Canada)

Austin TX - BookPeople
Dallas TX - Half-Price Books
Minneapolis MN - Wild Rumpus,
    Magers & Quinn Booksellers
    Birchbark Books and Native Arts
Atlanta GA - Atlanta Book Exchange,
    A Cappella Books
Washington DC - Politics and Prose
    Bookstore and Coffeehouse
Boston MA - Tatnuck Bookseller & Café,
    Brookline Booksmith

TIP: Seek and befriend your indie bookstore. Plan a party and/or your book launch. Indie bookstores have their own chatter lines. If your book is moving in one, others will hear.

Hook Up with IndieBound Bookstores

OUTSIDE OF AMAZON, IT'S going to be the independent bookstores that will support the local author ... I don't care if you are a self-publisher, indie publisher or you publish with a traditional publisher. Yes, they order through distributors, but ... and this is a BIG "but" ... in most cases, they are open to ordering directly from a publisher. If you are an indie publisher yourself, it takes a huge amount of pressure off you. It means you can get your books into their bookstores. Of course, it also means that you need to encourage/push buyers there as well.

TIP: The website to start your search is *www.IndieBound.org* AND include the IndieBound logo with a live link on your

website. Visitors will be connected to an indie bookstore in their zip code. Very cool.

The Big Chains Shouldn't Be Ignored

DID YOU KNOW THAT Barnes & Noble has a variety of programs that are ideal for the small press and independent book publisher? Make sure that you submit your titles to the:
Small Press Division, Barnes & Noble
122 Fifth Ave., New York, NY 10011.
Submit your completed book AND a Marketing Strategy. Remember: B&N and any other bookstore wants to know how you are going to drive buyers to their stores. Chat up social media, publicity, etc.

B&N has been a significant supporter of the Colorado Authors' Hall of Fame. Twice a year, my local bookstores sponsor bookfairs that have donated thousands of dollars to website development and scholarships for authors.

Plus, I've found that the stores are community oriented and supportive of local authors.

TIP: B&N has a very cool event called the Book Fair. Stores support groups that are nonprofits. If you are connected to one (or run one), contact the Community Relations Manager (CRM) at your local B&N—and ask if they run events there. What happens is that a percentage of book sales derived from customers who use the coupons that are provided will go back to your group.

This 'n That

Publishing requires a variety of needs, insights, tools and ahas to get on the success train. This 'n That delivers a lot of of information including images, one-sheets and audiobooks.

You Words Are Golden ... Speak Soon and Often

WHEN OTHERS LOVE YOUR book, or discover that it delivers a solution to a problem ... your voice is golden—use it. And get paid for it. Pay comes in the form of a speaking fee; it also comes in book sales. Better yet, do a combo.

Should you speak and not get paid?—maybe, maybe not. I've spoken professionally for three decades, meaning I got paid when I opened my mouth. Ninety percent of all my presentations had a speaking fee attached to them. The other 10 percent? Marketing.
And caring—my approach was that if I believed that there was someone in the audience that can hire me at my speaking fee, I would most likely speak at a reduced fee or for no fee. Or, if I felt passionate and was dedicated to the group,

I would always waive my fee. Otherwise, I got paid and my books were sold at the event. Over the years, anywhere from 30 to 50 percent of the audience bought a book after a presentation. Of that amount, half again bought a second book.

National groups can engage you as a speaker, so can local. There may be book clubs; there could be groups that in lieu of paying you, everyone buys a book; there could be groups that bring you in and include a copy of your book in the registration fee.

TIP: Combining speaking and authoring can create income that usually exceeds what most make working for others. Speak on your topic before your book is available—pre-sell copies. Contact groups that bring in speakers—both "fee" and "free." These group engagements are golden opportunities for your book sales. Create a Speaker One-Sheet that shines on your expertise and solution delivery.

Get it on your website and use it to mail/email to meeting planners and decision makers who plan programs. The sooner,

the better—don't wait until you have book in hand. And, *always* have your book with you and *always* carry a few cases in your car. As the Chief Marketing Officer, the product you are selling is called your book. You need to have it available at all times.

Always Get a Word Document of Your Final Book PDF

AFTER YOU HAVE YOUR book layed out by a designer, request that a file in addition to the final PDF of the book be created. The final book is always different from the edited manuscript you turned in for layout. Always. The post layout "cold eye" read before printing always finds additional changes. You want a "clean" new Word document in your master book file to make any additions, deletions to, for future print runs or revisions.

TIP: There are so many changes in a manuscript AFTER it is sent to a designer that it's hard to keep up with them. Ask what the costs are for a final conversion back to a Word document post PDF. That way—any

future editions are easy to work within and you have the "latest" to work on.

NEVER Assume Images Online Are Free

BEWARE OF COPYRIGHT INFRINGEMENT. Just because you found the perfect image or photo via a Google search doesn't mean you can do a copy/paste into your blog or book. Photos on Flickr, Fotolia, etc., have a range of rights— so make sure you're allowed to use an image before you download. Websites that offer images for use will include what usage is allowed and what the costs are. They also include a variety of forms that they can be downloaded in.

TIP: Be savvy and start creating your own images. Sources like *BookBrush.com, Canva.com* and *PicMonkey.com* are excellent tools to use. There are both free and for fee images on their sites.

Online images: NEVER Assume ...

Use Images That Are Royalty-Free for Your Book

IF YOU HAVE IMAGES on your cover or interior, make sure that they are royalty-free.

You may have to pay for the initial usage but that's it. Subscription websites for royalty-free and rights managed images are plentiful. Just because you found them on the Internet doesn't mean that they are free to use. Websites to check out that deliver royalty-free options include:

IStockPhoto.com   *CanStock.com*
Fotolia.com   *CorbisImages.com*
ThinkStockPhotos.com   *123rf.com*
DreamsTime.com   *BigStockPhoto.com*
ShutterStock.com   *OpenPhoto.net*
StockFreeImages.com   *Unprofound.com*

*PixelPerfectDigital.com   MorgueFile.com
Pixabay.com*

**TIP: Also, consider having an illustrator create your own images, like I've done throughout this book. They are mine.
I've paid for them and can use them again and again.**

If you use your images in posters, create a © watermark that includes your website. That way, if they are shared via the Internet (and most likely, they will be), you and your website get shared as well.

Get the Difference Between Net Discounted Pricing and Full Retail Pricing

YOU MAY THINK THAT you, as the publisher or owner of the book, control the price. Think again—your buyer plays a role ... as in how much is reasonable to pay. Price is a compromise of sorts. The full retail price is a suggested one. A consumer can negotiate or a distributor or distributors or wholesalers may dictate what they will pay you based on what you say the retail price is.

For example—most distributors/wholesalers in the book business will expect a 45 to 60 percent discount from the list price so it can in turn, resell the book. For your $15 book, you will receive $6 to$8 per book if sold. For

Amazon's Advantage account, it calculates what it pays you based on your initial retail price with a 55 percent discount. If it's $15 and Amazon decides to drop the price to $12.18 to the buyer, it won't affect your payout—it's still a net 0.45 of $15, or $6.

TIP: Make sure your book is competitively priced for your genre and industry and understand that there is an additional "cost" to doing business beyond actual book production, especially when others are attempting to resell your book.

Don't Forget Video: Book and Author Tip Sheets

NOW THAT YOU ARE creating Tips in writing, convert your words to a short Video Tip. Upload each tip video to your YouTube account. Include keywords/phrases in the video title and description. Author Virtual Assistant, Kelly Johnson (*CornerstoneVA.com*), suggests that you create a playlist to identify this "group" of videos as Tips on _____.

TIP: Share the videos on your social media (including Pinterest—you can pin YouTube videos on Pinterest boards).

Avoid AFS-Author Fatigue Syndrome: Get a Virtual Assistant

WHAT IS YOUR TIME worth? What do you love to do and what do you want to avoid like the plague? Start making a list and then open yourself up to hiring a "task doer" to bring some sanity to your authoring life. A Virtual Assistant—one that takes over the tasks you either don't have time to do, don't know how to do, or don't want to do—becomes a pain and stress releaser.

The more time authors spend on tasks that frustrate them or are not a strength, the more time authors are taking away from writing their book, marketing their book, building their brand, selling their book ... or just taking some time off.

Having a Virtual Assistant—a VA—may be one of the best investments you make. He or she may take over your social media; handle all the technology side; assist you with creating blogs, articles, newsletters, slides, flyers—you name it. Skills you need are all buyable. You want to partner with one that allows you to focus on your strengths and achieve successful results faster. And "partnering" is the right word. A VA becomes a sounding board for new ideas and new tools. The VA is at your side—whether across town or on the other side of the world.

TIP: Make sure you interview "deeply" for a VA you are interested in engaging. Get pricing; how does the VA work (does it match how you work); what's the VA's accessibility; what is his or her skill (knowing social media and technology are musts—the question is: what types of technology are a fit for what you do?); the VA should be adept in using Wordpress for your website. Before your interview, make a list of all the things you currently do that you would like to pass to another

to do for you (be reasonable—the VA isn't going to cook and clean).

As someone who has two VAs, I created a service with my company to help authors out. You can discover what the Author's Assistant can do here at *https://thebookshepherd.com/the-authors-assistant/*

I've done several podcasts on how to work with VAs. Here's one of my favorites from the *AuthorU-Your Guide to Book Publishing* radio show where Kelly Johnson, the Author's Virtual Assistant, is my guest: *http://bit.ly/AuthorVAs*.

It is loaded with "tips" on what to ask a potential VA in your interview.

Not Having Your Book Available in Multiple Formats

DON'T JUST CREATE A print book, an audiobook or an eBook. In many cases, all three are appropriate. At the minimum, your book should be available via the "p" format and the "e" format. Amazon's *Whispersync* program allows for the audiobook version to be read on eBook format—turn off audio, open "e" and your reading begins where your listening leaves off.

The great majority of book sales are for printed books. Why would you want only "e" ... creating an IngramSpark and/or KDP Kindle account and uploading your formatted book for print reading won't break your pocketbook and allows for all. Plus, you mark the box on

TIP: Many book buyers buy an additional format to the book. The savvy author plans for multiple streams for book buyers and book sales. Do digital books, but always create the companion print to go with it.

Don't Miss the Billion Dollar Audiobook Industry Publishing Option

IT IS BOOK MARKETING 101 to be everywhere your readers (and buyers) are. That means print, digital or "e" and audio. Too many authors either bypass doing an audiobook, or are ignorant of the audiobook option. Don't you be. Estimated to generate in excess of three billion dollars in total revenues for 2022 alone, it's a platform that can be entered without spending a fortune. According to Richard Rieman, author of *The Author's Guide to Audiobook Creation*, the production cost has dropped significantly. "In the late '90s, you would have been looking at $20,000 plus to create a professional audiobook. Today, you can bring it in for well under $3,000." That's huge! The explosion of localized studios is one reason; the other is there is the availability of creating your own home studio with sophisticated software and accessories that are user-friendly.

Amazon's "Whispersync" feature lets readers seamlessly move from the eBook version to the audiobook. When the listener stops on the audiobook and turns it off and then opens up the eBook hours, weeks, or even a month later, the eBook "knows" what sentence to begin with. How cool is that?

TIP: The major publishers usually create audiobooks for their books. One of the secrets for small press, independent publishers, or those who call themselves "self-publishers" is to create the audiobook. Having multiple options available tells the book buying world that you are a player, not a dabbler.

Get Richard Rieman's *The Author's Guide to Audiobook Creation* (it's a fast read with all the how-tos you need) to get audiobook smart. Ideally, you want print, eBook and audiobook to be available when you first launch. If it's an "add-on" post publication

of the other two, it gives you an opportunity to "relaunch" your book again announcing the variety of formats.

Most "how-tos" start off with the author's insights and tips about success. By avoiding or fixing the first 91 blunders, you are ready for the next level of success components. This section and the final #101: SuperFans and SuperReaders—Don't Lose Them ... Discover and Nourish Them *delivers the perfect wrapping for your publishing achievements.*

Delete People Who Don't Work with and for You

ALWAYS BE LOYAL TO your book and your vision ... don't let others tell you what you think ... don't let them seduce you into going down a path that doesn't feel right ... don't spend moneys that you don't have.

An editor needs to *get* your book; the illustrator needs to *express* what you see; the cover designer needs to be *current* with what's hot in the bookstores in style yet *expressive* with your topic/content; the interior designer needs to be able to do *more* than just lay out line after line of text; if you work with a content/developmental editor or ghost writer, it's critical that *your voice* is predominant, not his or hers; and if you have a book shepherd or consultant, it's essential that not only does he or she *get your book*, it's vital that he or she has all the *components* on his or her team to complement and complete your book project.

Fulfillment is important. Each of the individuals you engage has a commitment to you to deliver what they promised. But, and it's a *BIG but*, you have a commitment to them. As the author, you need—no, you *must*—deliver to each of them the book (or section) that they are to fine tune in the stage it needs to be in. If you don't, it delays production and increases costs.

TIP: Creating your book as a DIY project is usually a fatal mistake; keeping the wrong people on your team is equally so.

Not Branding Yourself as the Expert

AS THE AUTHOR, YOU are the expert. Wear it proudly and position yourself. You do it with your book; any presentations you make; with interviews and the media. Your expertise is integrated with your brand. Phrases, key buzz words and topics, designs, colors, affiliations all become part of your persona.

Branding is used within your book, on the covers (front and back), in your marketing material—everywhere! Branding is about you—all about YOU.

Lynn Hellerstein is an optometrist who specializes in vision therapy. She is the author of *See It. Say It. Do It!,* a book all about using visualization to achieve goals. It's presented as a tool that is highly interactive for parents to use to help their kids in areas like sports, math, music, reading, dealing with homework and tests. Using strong primary colors, a banner with the title was created that is woven throughout everything she does—her website, webinars she gives, media releases, articles, programs she presents—you name it; once you see it, you recognize it instantly.

When she started winning book awards, she tapped into the title and added, *See It. Say It. Do It! Did It!* When she sees a news item involving kids and sports, academics or music, she would reach out to the media source and offer her input as an expert.

Lynn was able to spin off an 8 x 11 workbook to match *See It. Say It. Do It!* and from that, another small, mini-book was created: *50 Tips to Improve Your Sports Performance* format. And each carries the banner branding created by Annie Harmon, her designer from the beginning.

TIP: Branding is like the peanut butter and jelly of marketing. You want to start it early and weave it through everything that you do. Not adding "expert" in your social media profiles, in your signature lines and any other articles, blogs, etc., that you release is a giant blunder.

What should that look like? Something like this: *Judith Briles is The Book Shepherd. She's an expert on publishing, book strategy, book marketing and crowdfunding for authors.* (124 characters with spaces). Or, *Dr. Judith Briles is an expert in publishing and a book strategist.* (68 characters with spaces). Or, *The Book Shepherd, Judith Briles is a publishing expert and book strategist.* (76 characters with spaces).

Learn what "space" you have—meaning word or character count and then fine tune your expert tag lines. Use and reuse across your social media profiles. For articles and blogs, you usually have more space—just add to it and don't forget contact info on website and email.

Embracing the Squirrel Factor Guarantees De-Focusing

WHEN YOU ARE IN the heart of your writing, your crowdfunding program, your marketing, your "anything to do with your book," you need to become myopic to succeed. Outside noise—from doing your love of the Garage Sale Saturday adventure to playing hooky for a weekend to diving into a thriller you have been dying to chew over aren't allowed.

The Squirrel Factor pulls you away at a moment's notice—it can be a lot of fun, taking you to places that you enjoy ... but, when you are on the author's quest, it can become the kiss of book death.

TIP: Get FOCUSED, pronto ... Think of an almost isolation situation—your loved ones can bring you food and drink—but stay out and away. You are the Author at Work.

Not Staying Visible

DON'T ASSUME BOOK BUYERS are going to find you ... you have to go to "*them*," don't wait for the phone to ring. Brand everything you do and become the expert in your marketplace; use Google Alerts; follow Blogs and Twitter accounts and make comments when appropriate; write articles that tie in with your book and place them on the Internet as well as in newsletters and magazines that your "crowd" reads or has a membership with; and, be generous—don't be afraid to use your book as a calling card ... meaning that you give it to people that you know who will spread the word (or hire you to speak).

By the time you've got your book in your hands, you will have your own list of "Note to self: next time, don't do this ..." I know this journey well, and at the top of mine is the "If I knew then what I know now ... I would have saved thousands of dollars, eliminated the confusion that the publishing maze creates and saved untold hours of time."

TIP: You will make mistakes; everyone does. The key is to learn, and not repeat.

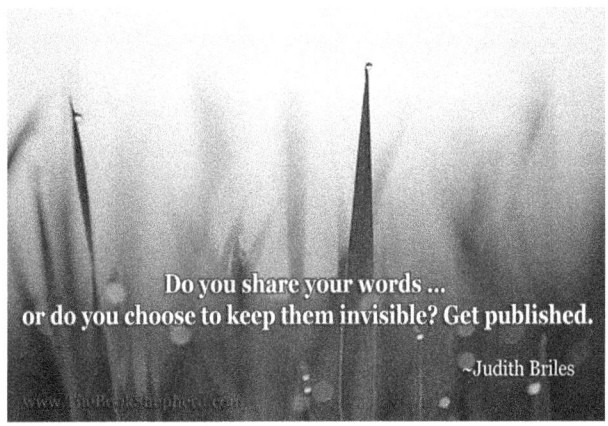

Claim Your Expertise ... the Sooner, the Better

BEING AN AUTHOR ISN'T the time to be shy ..., it's the time to shout out who and what you are/do. Yet too many authors fade into the shadows. Brand yourself as the expert in _____. Push it out in all your social media profiles. Create words and phrases that label you as the expert in _____. Your signature within your emails should include it as well as any copy that you put out that has your bio—be it long or short.

Join *Quora.com* and add your voice, experience and input to questions that pop up in your area of expertise.

TIP: The word "expert" is one of the top searched adjectives when someone is looking online for an authority or assistance. Add it to your keyword phrases and descriptors.

Avoid the RTP Syndrome ... Rush to Publish

TOO MANY AUTHORS RUSH into publishing without understanding the many hurdles and obstacles. What happens is you set yourself up for the publishing predators; getting into things and forking over moneys that you shouldn't have; and going down rabbit holes you should never have fallen into.

TIP: Breathe and start learning. Pre-work can start in a bookstore. From learning about what books are in vogue at bookstores; what cover designs are current; what formats are best for you and your genre/specialty on the Internet. Get involved with a community of authors who see authoring as a business versus a hobby. Join *AuthorU.org* to fast-forward you.

Webinars are available daily on the Internet (caution: most have a goal to sell you something ... you don't have to buy); so are teleseminars; blogs are everywhere—*PublicityHound.com, TheBookDesigner.com, SocialMediaExaminer.com, AuthorU.org, TheBookShepherd.com, 1106Design.com, JohnKremer.com, DanielHallPresents.com*—extending free multiple offerings throughout the week; conferences that include strategy, book marketing, the how-tos of publishing (AuthorU does a three-day *Extravaganza* with a trade show every September). The bottom line is that there is plenty of information available. Start learning about publishing and commit to a practice of staying current. The publishing landscape will continue to change. Social media and the Internet have become the driving gamechangers.

Know How You Are Going to Get Paid ... Including if Royalties Are Part of the Deal

IF YOU ARE YOUR own publisher, you should know your costs. If you don't, start crunching your numbers. Knowing your break-evens and when profitability enters your publishing sphere is essential.

If you are publishing via a "self-publishing" company, *author beware* surfaces. Royalties are bantered about—often in a confusing manner—sometimes even stating on websites that they can't be determined until trim size and page count is in place. Nonsense. Clarify exactly what you will NET on each book sold. If the company can't be specific, *run*, don't walk away from working with this company.

If it's a traditional publisher, royalty payments are spelled out within a clause in your contract.

TIP: Traditional publishers pay on the net amount of a book sale based on the total sales the book has achieved, usually twice a year; self-publishing companies each have their own formulas—if you are unclear, get an outside opinion.

If you are selling via Amazon Advantage or Market Place or IngramSpark, their percentages are clearly stated in their agreements. If you are only selling via your website or "back of room" ... you should know what your profit margins are.

Shout Out Your Sayings and Quotes

IF YOU ARE WRITING nonfiction, most likely your book is peppered with quotable sayings, quotes, ahas, key concepts, solutions, etc. If it's fiction, do your characters have quotable sayings, quotes, ahas, key concepts, solutions, etc.? They can be kickbutt, funny or just something to noodle on. Are you making "art" out of them? Are they graphically attractive to the eye? If not, it's a blunder you don't want to keep doing.

Create posters and clips that you can push out via social media. Create posters—both plain and with images—that you can use within blogs and post alone on your social media platforms. Create a Board on Pinterest that you can add to and then link to your other social media platforms. People like quotes; there are zillions of books just on quotes. Mine are published in a gift book: *Snappy Sassy Salty: Wise Words for Authors & Writers* that has more than 250 of my favorites that I've created through the years from working with authors. They are routinely repeated in my Twitter and Facebook posts. I also have two Pinterest Boards: one is dedicated to my own quotes; the other is dedicated to quotes I love that I've found from others.

TIP: *Canva* is an excellent tool to use to create posters and banners. Do at least two versions: plain, maybe with some type of textured background or border; the other with an image—a photo of your own, something you've found that is "free," or one that you've paid for.

Don't forget to add your own copyright mark on them. All mine have ©The Book Shepherd or ©Judith Briles, The Book Shepherd. They get copied and recirculated—why not have your name/brand carried along as it travels?

Create Tip Sheets and Cheat Sheets

AUTHORS DON'T MAXIMIZE THEIR hot advice ... yet readers love the idea of getting them in a nugget format. Enter the Tip or Cheat Sheet.

For nonfiction, go through the chapters—what can you pull from them to create a Top 10 or How-to List of Tips and Tricks ... you get the picture. For the fiction crowd, your tips could be created for other writers. A twist could be to create a Tip or Cheat Sheet on how to dig out the villain from a writer's hints—use your imagination. What do your inquiring readers want to know?

TIP: Tip and Cheat Sheets are short cuts and ahas. They are great to use on your website as a lure to attract followers and gather emails.

At the back of each of the *AuthorYOU MIni-Guides*, a Cheat Sheet is included (you will find it on page 309).

An add for you is that a Cheat Sheet can serve as a stand-alone blog. Or, you can take each "Cheat" and create a separate blog out of it. It becomes a "repurpose."

101

SuperFans and SuperReaders–Don't Lose Them … Discover and Nourish

SUPERFANS ARE THE SECRET sauce to author success. What is a SuperFan? Anyone who buys and devours every book you write—just your name on it, it means there's a sale to your fan. SuperFans create the "buzz club" for you—they will encourage others to buy your book(s). And, they follow you on social media and your blog. Meaning, you have their names and emails.

If you put out that your "next" book is available for pre-sale, they pre-order it. If you ask for shout-out help when your book launches, they are there to push it out with you, in your marketing efforts. If a "troll" or jerk attacks you on social media, they become your defenders. SuperFans are invaluable. They can assist you in your marketing efforts, even at signings; they can serve as beta readers for your next book. And they can provide social media proof with their comments on your blogs and to others that you are the cat's meow.

TIP: Finding them, nurturing them and delivering for them takes work. They are hungry for the next book. Start with knowing your genre inside and out. Typically, SuperFans will browse the Top-100 Paid and Top-100 Free lists in their preferred Amazon genres. Google will become your best friend as you begin your SuperFan quest.

- **Explore there and create a list of keywords and key phrases that form the mental "tags" of your genre. Build a list of tags. You will use these in hashtags as well.**

- **Next, join an Internet book club (or discover one via your favorite local bookstore—most know who they are for a variety of genres). This is to be a participant and observer ... NOT to boast about your own book.**

- **Then, identify and use trending hashtags popular with your target genre. When the new *Star Wars* movie popped, the #TheForceAwakens was a hot trending hashtag. Make it a habit to use them in all your social media posts.**

- **Do a search for the "best online <your genre name> reader communities." Explore them to determine which are worth engaging with.**

- **Do a search for and follow the most popular book review blogs in your genre.**

When you identify SuperReaders, your goal is to now convert them to SuperFans—yours. You will by reaching out—are they already in a group you belong to? Within the groups, don't be shy. Ask for beta readers: feedback on book cover samples (this is a great way to stir up interest—remember, you aren't selling anything, just asking for feedback); offer sneak previews of "polished"chapters; and you can even ask for an in-person meeting if it's feasible. Send out tips of the week if you are a nonfiction author around your book and/or expertise. For fiction authors can share about the geography, history, even character dilemmas. Consider having Super-Readers "vote" on photos for what characters should look like—even naming the villain.

Build your community and invite your readers in. Create contests; have them vote on cover choices. One of my favorites was when a cookbook client did a worst apron contest—another did the best of the worst dinner disasters. Of course, pictures were required to enter with a prize for the "best" from each. For all, thank them publicly and do feature the winner's photo.

Be willing to reveal yourself. SuperFans want to know about you—what your hobbies are; what inspires you to write; what blocks you and how you get untangled; if you have pets; what you do for fun; what you are working on next. Share items that create a bridge between you and your SuperFans.

As you build your mostly online relationships, you want to give them a "reason to buy" your book. Think premiums—signed bookmarks, signed books, limited hardcover editions,

printed card recipes for cookbooks, nonfiction books may have worksheets or flow sheets you sell separately, you may even throw in a special Skype chat. Use your imagination.
A SuperFan community dedicated to you and your books will ensure book sales and author happiness.

One More Thing ...

EVEN IF YOU BELIEVE you are error free (Really?), it's wise to review the 101 blunders, bloopers and boo-boos. Why? Because we all need to be goosed ... reminded that some of the obvious can get lost when there is so much on the author plate. It's easy to let items slide or just simply forget something that we know or heard about, but somehow the overload or overwhelm factor got in the way of executing them.

Publishing a book is exciting. As one physician client said as we moved to the stage of the final cold-eye read and getting print bids: "You are right, it is like giving birth and we are at eight centimeters."

Nodding my head, I added, "Yes, and now the final push happens. When your baby is birthed, you have to teach it to crawl, walk and run." Be ready to lose some sleep: book babies sometimes need around the clock feeding and nurturing.

Writing a book is the easy part. It's learning the business, how to market, how to promote and how to stay enthused … that's the work.

Here's to you and your publishing success!

Publishing Blunder, Blooper, Boo-Boo Cheat Sheet

1. Make a sign: **Perfection is the enemy of the author.** Post it where you can see it. Perfection is a form of procrastination. If you keep trying to make it "perfect" ... time disappears into a vacuum, as does opportunity.

2. **Opportunity windows can close quickly**—when you constantly edit, re-edit, rewrite, "re" anything, windows can close. Stay away from the "one for the money; two for show; three to get ready; three to get ready; three ... to ... get ... ready practices that so many authors-to-be engage in.

3. **Don't get swayed by someone dangling a "contract" in front of you**—check it out. Contracts are usually written for the "best

interests" of the person or company sending it to you. Make sure you have escape clauses. Don't sign anything that uses a phrase like: "This contract can be terminated in 30 days if both parties mutually agree." The phrase "mutually agree" is your deal killer.

4. **Book selling is highly competitive.** If your book:
    1: doesn't visually compete with other books in your genre (cover and interior design) and
    2: hasn't been professionally edited ... "they will know."

    Who are "they"?—your buyers and reviewers. And they tell others. That's an *oh-oh.* In other words, get book professionals in play from the get-go.

5. **Do the online and brick and mortar bookstore cover test.** Go into any bookstore and go to the area your book would be carried in. Look at every competing book. How does yours compare/compete in looks and presentation? Now, go to the front of the store and check out all the new arrivals. What are the colors? Fonts used in titles? What do the interiors look like? Are there images?

You are doing "competitive book spy" work.
You want your book to look, feel, be like
what the major publishers are putting out.
In your spy work, is there anything that
you love. Take a picture and get it to your
designer. Can he or she incorporate some
of the ideas that "sing" to you for your
book?

6. **You need Amazon.** Get over that it takes
   a hefty percentage—so does any book
   wholesaler, distributor and retailer. Get
   over it. Join the Amazon.com/Advantage
   program for publishers. Join Author
   Central—it's the secret sauce to get a
   "live" person within seconds at Amazon
   for help.

7. **Get your "front matter" and "back
   matter" organized.** Don't bombard your
   reader-to-be with a page load of fillers in
   the front matter before your book content
   unfolds. Yes—you need a Title page,
   Copyright page, and Contents page if it's a
   nonfiction book (dump the "table of")—
   these are must haves. Nice to add Dedication
   page, "Praise" for your book from "names"
   who are giving short endorsements (you
   would do this in the first page or two

when the cover is opened) and if there is a Foreword or Preface. Then STOP ... roll into the contents of the book.

It was common for Acknowledgments to be in the front. Today it's more common to roll them to the "back matter" ... after your book has given its last bit of advice or ended your awesome story.

8. **Do the "ask for book review" in your book ... as in writing ... you want shout outs posted!** Don't be shy; tell your readers you need their support. Put your "ask" in writing, in the front matter if there is a "note from the author"; you could even wedge it in if they liked your novel, poem, solutions—even the design of the book—to post it on Amazon and Goodreads.

9. **Don't forget about YOU!** Add **About the Author** and if you consult, speak—do any type of presentations, have a business, create a **How to Work with ME** page (please put your name here—not ME). Include short descriptors of what you do and don't forget: contact info—website, email, phone number and include your preferred social media channels that you

would like them to follow. And, add a photo ... ideally a different one on each page.

10. **Put a hex on the RTP Syndrome.** I know, I know ... you want your book out. But the book you want out should be one that you have zero regrets about. Get the editing done; get a professional cover and interior designer on your team. Don't rush it. The RTP Syndrome is the Rush to Publish scenario. If you put out something that is loaded with errors, "they" will know ... the "they" being your potential Fans. Then "they" tell others ... the book is mediocre.

11. **Before you finalize your cover design ...** reduce it to a 25 percent size. The thumbnail that Amazon will post on its site. Does it pop? Can you see the title? The image? You want your book cover to pop out on the page.

12. **Commit, Commit, Commit.** Plan your Launch Timeframe. Celebrate and take a bow!

Thanks to My Village

SOME BOOKS COME TO authors over what seems like an eternity of time; others come roaring in like a lion. *How to Avoid Book Publishing Blunders* had to happen. In fact, it's been long overdue.

Originally, this book bubbled up while I was teaching the *How to Write a Book in 4 Weeks* course in my hometown of Denver, Colorado—a course I now offer online as well. Leading and teaching the class, it made sense that I too would write a book and demonstrate in a hands-on approach that I could deliver what I preached. Initially, I had planned on 50 blunders and began to pull them together. The rewrites took a bit longer than I planned. It wasn't my priority, after all; I had clients' books to work on. Then I started tweaking. Of course, I would add a "goose" to each item I identified—a what to do next. The TIP. Then, I got the idea—what the heck, let's shoot for 100. My mini-book is bigger than the others in the *AuthorYOU Mini-Guide* series—you see, there was so much material in my years of book shepherding to pull from! You get 101 PLUS within the narratives and Tips—they total over 200!

I reached out to respected colleagues and publishing professionals for their sage advice and hiccups they routinely see: Helen Sedwick, Patti Thorn, Michele DeFlippo, Kelly Johnson, Phil Knight, Nick Zelinger, Joan Stewart, Joel Friedlander, Tom Campbell, Brian Jud, Bret Ridgway and Rebecca Finkel, and of course, my book shepherding clients. In many cases, they are the walking talking survivors of many blunders, bloopers and boo-boos.

In the late summer of 2015, my publishing comrade and long-time friend Dan Poynter and I had one of our hour plus phone calls sharing our "greatest hit blunders" ... many are threaded throughout. I miss him—as thousands of others do—with his passing.

As The Book Shepherd, at times, I am amused, alarmed and downright appalled at some of the repeated mistakes authors create themselves or allow themselves to get sucked into. This needed to be a book, not a huge one, but one that is not GeekSpeak or loaded with charts and graphs—a how-to book that is easy to understand and loaded with practical tips and guidance.

As with the other books in the *AuthorYOU Mini-Guide* series, the format had to say *fun*. You get a book with big solutions and ideas. To bring a small book to life, the team came together again in the first round of emails.

Thank you to the awesome Nick Zelinger of NZGraphics. I can only the fingers on one hand to identify book and cover designers who are as flexible as Nick is. "Sure, why not, let's see what we can do this time with those sheepie guys of yours." Love what he continues to do.

Thank you to my other favorite cover and book designer Rebecca Finkel. When it was time for the "do over" of the series, her vision for the covers was perfecto!

Thank you to Leah Dasalla, who took my sheepie guys and made a series of posters and banners to flow throughout the book. "This has been a fun project. Are you going to do another one like it?" Yes I am—it's the next in the *AuthorYOU Mini-Guide* series.

Thank you to Kelly Johnson, my favorite Geek Girl, who can do just about anything behind the scenes ... and take center stage when need be. "I love those sheepie guys ... they always make me smile." As they do me.

Thank you to Don Sidle, the sheepie guy creator. Coming back for a fifth book appearance, the sheep family has had quite a journey. "I like whimsy and goofy—you inspired me to bring the sheep out!" Who would have thought that sheep would become part of my branding and who would have thought of adding a wheel chair, crutches and a boo-boo arm to the mix? Don did.

Thank you to my first line editor, John Maling, who does the tweaking in rewrites—"are you sure you really want to say it this way?" "This is much needed ... it's simple enough, limits the overwhelm and eliminates the unknown. I like it." Always helps when your editor "likes" the book!

Thank you to Peggie Ireland, my cold-eye editor who always catches things my eyes can no longer see and my head knows have already been fixed, and haven't been. "I love these practical, hands-on books." Me too—I think I know what the next one is ... then another pops up.

t takes a village to create a book. It takes a village to keep an author going. And it takes a village to be successful in your book publishing. I am blessed to have my awesome village. Find yours and take care of it.

Meet Judith Briles

The Book Shepherd

About the Author

MEET DR. JUDITH BRILES, known as The Book Shepherd, Author and Publishing Expert, Book Publishing and Crowdfunding Coach, Conference Speaker, Radio Host and the Founder and Chief Visionary Officer of *AuthorU.org*, a membership organization created for the author who wants to be seriously successful. She's been writing about and conducting workshops on publishing since the '80s and coordinates the annual *Publishing at Sea* working cruise conferences.

Judith is the author of 42 books—18 published with New York houses until she created Mile High Press in 2000. Based in Colorado, she's published in 17 countries and with more than a 1,000,000 copies sold of her work. *How to Create Snappy Sassy Salty Success for Authors and Writers* joined her multi-award winning bestseller, *Author YOU: Creating and Building Your Author and Book Platforms. Author YOU* was selected as a Book of the Year in the Writing|Publishing category at the IndieFab awards and is considered the must have workbook for Platform building.

How to Avoid Book Publishing Blunders is the third book in the *AuthorYOU Mini-Guide* series joining *How to Create Crowdfunding Success for Authors & Writers and The Authors Guide to AudioBook Creation* by Richard Rieman. *How to Create a Million Dollar Speech* and *The Author's Walk* are now members of her publishing family.

Judith has chaired numerous publishing conferences and is a frequent speaker at writer and publishing conferences. She knows publishing and she gets the challenges that authors go through in creating and publishing their books. Known as The Book Shepherd to many, she's personally guided hundreds of publishing clients throughout the United States, Canada, Mexico, Australia and Hong Kong.

Throughout the year, she presents her Judith Briles Unplugged events. Over two days, strategies and how-to are delivered for: Book Publishing, Book Marketing, Social Media, or Speaking.

All details are under the Experiences tab on her website.

Follow @*AuthorU* and @*MyBookShepherd* on Twitter and do a "Like" at AuthorYOU and Judith Briles-The Book Shepherd on Facebook. Join the AuthorYOU LinkedIn group and the Book Publishing with The Book Shepherd group on Facebook To book a consult with Judith, you can secure a 30-minute or 60-minute slot at: *https://TheBookShepherd.com/pick-judiths-brain/* or go to her website.

Since inception, authors have downloaded over 9 million episodes of AuthorU-Your Guide to Book Publishing podcast. Access it on iTunes at as well as through her website or at *http://bit.ly/AuthorURadio*.

Speaking and Book Shepherding are what Judith does. If you want to create a book that has no regrets or bring her to your conference, contact her at *Judith@Briles.com*.

© 2016 All rights reserved. Judith Briles, The Book Shepherd

Working with Judith

Judith Briles Consults and Speaks ... Would You Like to Listen, Learn, Publish?

Judith Briles would be delighted to participate in your publishing conference or to speak to your group. For Book Shepherding and Book Consulting, email or call her offices. If you want a highly interactive, informative and fun presentation or workshop, call or email her for availability:

Judith Briles
JudithBriles.com
Judith@TheBookShepherd.com
www.TheBookShepherd.com
303-885-2207
Consulting by the Hour or by the Project

Workshops and Keynotes include: *Is There a Book in You?, CrowdFunding Your Book Project, Create Ninja Book Marketing, Avoid the Blunders that Can Sink Your Book, Boring Speeches Suck! ... Create a Talk that Sells Thousands of Books and Can Make Over $1,000,000, Create Your Author* *and Book Platforms, Creating Confidence as an Author & Writer, If Publishing Is in Your Midst ... Which Option is for YOU and YOUR Book?, Stop the Social Media Insanity*

You want information and resources to help you sell books. My blogs, radio shows that are available in podcasting format and social media accounts are right up your alley in supplying information for today's author. Let's get connected:

The Book Shepherd Daily
http://tinyurl.com/TBSDaily

Blog
TheBookShepherd.com website

http://bit.ly/BookPublishingPodcast

Radio - iTunes Podcast Feed
http://toginet.com/rss/itunes/AuthorUYourGuideToBookPublishing

Instagram
Instagram.com/judith.thebookshepherd

Pinterest
JudithBriles

Twitter
@MyBookShepherd

LinkedIn
LinkedIn/in/judithbriles/

Facebook
Judith Briles

The Book Shepherd
facebook.com/TheBookShepherd

FB Group: Publishing with The Book Shepherd
facebook.com/groups/BookPublishingHelp

The AuthorYou Mini-Guide Series

How to Create Snappy Sassy Salty Success for Authors and Writers is the perfect pick-me-up for the aspiring author; for the author who has landed in a rut; or just a bit of inspiration.

How to Create a Million Dollar Speech delivers the secret sauce for book sales and turning an author's wisdom and expertise into the golden ticket.

How to Create Crowdfunding Success for Authors and Writers offers the latest up-to-date information on how successful crowdfunding campaigns can work for you.

How to Avoid Book Publishing Blunders gives you 101 gems of book publishing wisdom—essential reading for all authors wishing to self-publish.

New from Judith Briles:

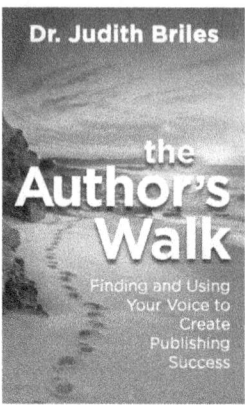

More inspiration and expert guidance from bestselling author and author advocate Judith Briles.

More of What They're Saying ...

Here's what I love about Judith Briles and this book: She gives it to you straight. No coddling. No B.S. She's the poster child for self-publishing tough love. Judith knows what will make a positive difference for authors and shares it in this gem that I will recommend to every author who asks me, "What do I need to know about publishing my book?"
—Sandra Beckwith, *BuildBookBuzz.com*

Judith Briles knows her audience for sure! This guidebook perfectly encapsulates the questions we authors who write to help authors succeed get asked most often. And no one knows the answers better the Briles!
—Carolyn Howard-Johnson,
author of the multi award-winning
How To Do It Frugally Series of books for writers

Whether you are a first-time or veteran author, the lessons shared in this book will serve you well to avoid mistakes that not only cost you money but also your time and energy.

Each time I went through the book, I found helpful reminders of essentials to have on my checklist for writing and publishing, and I discovered new tips to help keep me on track to avoid book publishing blunders.

Judith is a master at presenting information in an easy-to-implement manner to ensure authors achieve success.

Authors and publishers—you will find yourself returning again and again to this gem of a resource!"

—Kelly Johnson,
Owner, Cornerstone Virtual Assistance,
Specializes in working with authors

"This looks and is BRILLIANT! LOVE the cover, love the graphics throughout, love the contents, the layout. And this is SO timely! Judith hits another home run!"

—Mara Purl, author of *What the Heart Knows*

"This book will help you avoid the most common book-publishing blunders. Each concise point delivers the most important information you need on the subject – with tips showing you how to implement them. Judith's brilliance will help you sell more books more profitably."

—Brian Jud, author of *How to Make Real Money Selling Books* and Executive Director of the Association of Publishers for Special Sales

This easy-to-read guide can help you avoid the mistakes that many new authors make. The world of publishing can be overwhelming, but it doesn't have to be that way. Do yourself a favor and read this so you can be well-prepared before your book is released!

—Stephanie Chandler,
NonfictionAuthorsAssociation.com

www.ingramcontent.com/pod-product-compliance
Lightning Source LLC
Chambersburg PA
CBHW070907030426
42336CB00014BA/2323